The Tinder Box

A Play with Music for Children

Peter Whelan

A SAMUEL FRENCH ACTING EDITION

SAMUEL FRENCH

FOUNDED 1830

SAMUELFRENCH-LONDON.CO.UK
SAMUELFRENCH.COM

THE TINDER BOX

First performed at the New Victoria Theatre, North Staffordshire, on 30th November, 1994, with the following cast:

The Soldier	Daniel Tomlinson
The Witch	Katy Stephens
The King	Roger Delves-Broughton
The Queen	Kate Layden
The Princess	Biddy Wells
The Lady-in-waiting	Shelly Willets
Boots	Sarah Malin
Mrs Pin	Stephanie Jacobs
Twist	Steven Granville
Scoff	John Wild

Other parts taken by members of the company

Directed by Peter Cheeseman
Design and Costumes by Lis Evans
Lighting by Paul W Jones
Sound by James Earls-Davis
Music by Peter Whelan, John Kirkpatrick and James Earls-Davis
Arrangements and Musical Direction by John Kirkpatrick

CHARACTERS

Narrators (2 or more)
Soldier
Comrade
Witch
Dog (with eyes as big as saucers) ⎫
Dog (with eyes as big as millwheels) ⎪ See note,
Dog (with eyes as big as the round ⎬ below
   towers of Copenhagen) ⎭
King
Queen
Princess Sigrid
Lady-in-waiting
Officer
Beggar
2nd Officer
Rose Seller
Baker
Boots
Mrs Pin
Scoff
Twist
Croupier
One-legged Beggar
Widow
Waiter
Cabaret Singer
Vicar
Woman
2nd Woman
Hangman
Townspeople, Servants, Night-club customers, etc.

The First Dog is the only speaking role. In the original
production, the First Dog was played by an actor in a suit,
the Second Dog was played by two actors in a larger suit,
and the Third Dog was represented by huge eyes that
descended from the heavens. The Second and Third Dogs
are not therefore, strictly speaking, "characters", although
the text treats them as such.

ACT I

A dusty road in Denmark. Evening

Church bells are ringing. The Narrators begin the story. As they do, the Soldier and his Comrade enter. The Soldier plays a drum, Comrade a fife. They are weary but in happy spirits

Narrators In a land called Denmark across the sea,
On a dusty road to a great city,
The church-bells ringing the end of the war,
A Soldier came marching, tired and sore,
With his Comrade-in-arms, his dearest friend,
Happy their battles were at an end;
And the Soldier drummed as they sang their song,
For the war had been cruel and the years had been long ...

The Narrators disappear

Song: It's Over

Soldier and Comrade (*singing*)
It's over! It's over!
Our fighting days are gone.
It's over. The war is over.
We don't know who's lost or won!
It's over. It's over.
We've given up the gun.
Fall out! Stand at ease!
Have a bite of bread and cheese,
It's over, and done.

As the song ends they arrive at a crossroads

Soldier (*speaking*)
This is the crossroads. You and I must part ...
Comrade I'm sorry, dear friend. I take it much to heart.

Soldier	Well we've been through some dangers me and you —
	When the cannons roared and the bullets flew.
Comrade	You stood by me then. I won't ever forget.
Soldier	Cheer up! You've wife and child waiting for you yet.
	Not like me, going to town all on my own ...
Comrade	Yes but marriage takes your money, Hans ——
Soldier	I'll give you a loan ... (*He takes some money from a pouch*)
Comrade	No!
Soldier	Yes! I've no-one to spend it on but me ... (*He takes a long dried sausage from his pack*)
	And you'll need some food for your long journey.
Comrade	But that's your last sausage!
Soldier	(*pushing the sausage in Comrade's belt*)
	Very true ...
Comrade	(*breaking it in half and giving half back*)
	Half and half ... like we always used to do.
Soldier	(*holding it up; ceremoniously*)
	The last sausage!

He blows the last post, imitating the trumpet. Then they eat, saving a piece for later

Comrade	So. Off I go home to my little farm ...
Soldier	Where you'll have your loved ones to keep you warm.
	It's the end of the summer. The cold's in the air.
	The leaves'll be falling — and you'll be snug there ...
Comrade	Well why not get married when you get to town?
Soldier	Yes — I fancy a lady in a velvet gown ...
Comrade	No! To a good, sweet woman who'll treat you well.
Soldier	Till she changes her mind and starts giving me hell!
Comrade	You've a rough tongue, dear Hans, but you'll change I daresay.

The Soldier gets his drum ready

Soldier	Come on! And I'll drum you along your way.

The Soldier beats the drum and they sing "It's Over"

Comrade marches out of sight along the road

The Soldier stops drumming and addresses the children in the audience:

(*Speaking*) There he goes. He's my friend and I bet we never meet again. Didn't invite me to his farm, did he? And d'you know why? It's too poor.

He's ashamed of it. Well, I've done my usual stupid thing. I've given him all my money and half my food ... except for this old stick of liquorice root I keep tied to my scabbard. Nice to have a chew in battle. Stops your teeth rattling. Now—I thought I was going to sleep in a bed tonight, but it seems I'm back in the open ... (*He singles out a child to talk to*) Ever slept in the open? I mean outside — not in a tent — under the open sky, the vault of heaven? Wonderful! You have to find a nice spot, though. I'll march on a bit ... (*He beats the drum and marches across the stage, then stops*) There's a good ditch over there ... but I think it's got rats. Take my advice — never sleep with rats. They won't keep still. Fidget all night. Very restless, rats. Hedgehogs are all right — as long as they keep to their side. They snore though. (*Pointing*) See there! A snake. Don't sleep with snakes. They keep up a sort of low hiss all night — not the full hiss — a half hiss, on and on. You keep waking up thinking someone's left the tap on. Which is stupid since there are no taps. (*He yawns*) Well, I'll have to find somewhere.

Music. The stage darkens a little. A hollow oak tree appears as there is a dissolve to:

SCENE 2

Soldier Look at that! An oak tree! Nice to sleep under an oak. Of course you have to put up with things dropping on you ... (*He unfolds his bedroll and spreads it by the tree*) Four-legged things ... Six-legged ... Eight-legged ... Thirty-two-legged — centipedes, I mean. You know centipedes have thirty-two legs not a hundred legs, don't you? They're very good dancers, centipedes. Not many people know it because whenever they see a centipede they go: "Eaagh! It's a centipede! Gerrroff!" Whereas they should say: "What luck — a centipede! Ask it to dance ... " (*He curls up in the blanket and pulls the drum near him*) My drum'll have to be my companion now. I'd never part from this drum ... (*He yawns*) He was shot once — see these patches? The bullet went in there — and out there. (*He yawns*) At the battle of ... of ... (*He puts his head down and sleeps*)

The stage darkens. There is the tap, tap, tap of a stick, off, as the Witch approaches. Music. Her shadow falls across the stage

The Witch enters and sees the Soldier right away. She stops

Silence. Suddenly, the Soldier sits bolt upright with a shout, as though from a nightmare

What was that?

Witch	It was me, soldier — just tapping my stick.
Soldier	You're a witch!
Witch	No I'm not ....
Soldier	You're in league with Satan ... The Devil ... Old Nick!
Witch	Oh come now! You don't believe in that stuff ...
Soldier	You're a witch, for I swear you're ugly enough.
Witch	Now is that kind? Now d'you think that's fair?
	I'm just an old lady, enjoying the evening air.
Soldier	Evening? This is the middle of the night!
Witch	Well, as you say, I'm not a pretty sight.
	So when I go for a walk it's with the moon and the stars,
	So folk don't have to see me.
	Well! You're back from the wars.
Soldier	I am.
Witch	Good. Would you like to do a job for me?
	It needs a soldier — and you're that I can see,
	Look at your knapsack and your handsome sword ——

Before the Soldier can stop her, the Witch draws his sword and holds it high. He tries to get it back as she taunts him:

	— Shall I tell you where all the money in the world is stored?
Soldier	Give me that!

She hands back the sword

	Now show me and I'll follow ...
Witch	The way's through this ancient oak. It's hollow.
	I can't go. I'm a frail old woman, not strong like you.
	But you can do it. Climb up and lower yourself through.
	I'll tie this rope your waist about ...
	And when you want to come back, I'll pull you out!

She produces a long length of rope from under her cloak and ties it round him

Soldier	I thought you weren't strong ...
Witch	Oh — I can help a bit.
Soldier	So, what do I do in the tree?
Witch	Well, that's it!
	Take all the money you want — all you can hold,
	In copper and silver and shining gold ...
Soldier	Go on ...
Witch	Climb down — and down — and under the ground,

A bright hall with three big doors is found.
Open the first door. The key's in the lock ...
I'll tell you what's in there to lessen the shock.
A great big chest with a dog sitting on it,
His eyes as big as saucers — but don't run from it.
Just spread my apron on the floor ... (*She gives him her apron*)
And he'll be so tame you could shake his paw.
In the chest, copper coins, take all you crave,
But if it's silver you want, you'll have to be brave ...
For in the next room is a dog bigger still,
With eyes as big as the wheels of a mill.
Show him the apron. You can open the chest.
Take the silver — unless it's gold you like best.
If so, in the third room, there's more than you could bargain ...
A dog with eyes as big as the round towers of Copenhagen!

Soldier   (*to the audience, explaining*)
That's the capital of Denmark — if you hadn't already guessed
at it. (*He thinks*)
But if the eyes are that big — how big is the rest of it?

Witch   Are you afraid?

Soldier   No!

Witch   I said it needed a soldier ... Did I speak true?

Soldier   All right ... I get the money?

Witch   Yes.

Soldier   So — what's in it for you?

Witch   I don't want money. You have to hide it.
I don't like locks.
All I want is my grandmother's tinder box.

Soldier   Tinder box?

Witch   When my grannie was a little girl,
She went down there — and got in such a whirl;
She was afraid of the dogs and left it behind.
If you could bring it up, it would be so kind.

Soldier   Her tinder box?

Witch   Yes.

Soldier   And that's all?

Witch   It's a bit of the past that I like to recall.
You're laughing at me — my sentimental ways ...
But it's something of *hers*, that I'll treasure always.

Soldier   All right. All right. I'll get it. I'm ready.

Witch   Climb up the tree and hold yourself steady.
You won't want those. Leave your drum and pack.

Soldier   Make sure they're here when I get back.
                Here goes! Into the tree ...

He exits into the tree, pulling the rope after him

Witch   (*calling after him, harshly*)
                And whatever you do, bring the tinder box to me!

She exits and the tree moves off

Music

*The Narrators appear. They speak almost musically, "harmonizing" by
alternating their timbre, pitch and intensity*

Narrators   Down through the dark of the hollow tree.
                Down through the twisting trunk of oak.
                Down through the hairy roots went he ...
                And the echoes round him spoke ... spoke ... spoke ...

There is a dissolve to:

SCENE 3

The Soldier is revealed in a lamp-lit hall, connected to the rope

Narrators   But soon a glimmer from below ...
                And all at once the soldier knew
                That this was the hall with the lamps aglow ...
                The Witch's tale was coming true!
Soldier This must be the "bright lit hall" she spoke of. All those lamps! How
        did it all get here, under the earth? And look! There's the three doors she
        talked about ... (*Miming*) One ... Two ... Three. Well, soldier. Into the first ...
        (*He mimes turning the key and entering*)
Narrators   Slowly, slowly, he turned the key;
                Hard against the door he pressed ....

The Dog with eyes as big as saucers appears, guarding a copper chest

                And saw the strangest dog you'd ever see,
                Guarding a copper chest!

The Narrators disappear

Soldier Hallo! What do they feed you on then? You are a handsome fellow ... (*To the audience*) I'll show him the Witch's apron.

The Dog makes an echoing "mmmmaammmm" sound that could be friendly — or not. The Soldier gulps. He lays down the apron

(*To the audience*) She was right. Each eye as big as s-a-saucer ...

The Dog rolls his eyes. We hear mystical sounds

(*To the Dog*) Come on ... I want to shake your paw, sir.

We hear more magical breathing dog sounds. The Dog gets off the chest and gets on to the apron. He solemnly lifts a paw. The Soldier shakes it

Just as she said! Now I can open the chest ... Can I? ... Yes?

The Dog nods and rolls his eyes. The Soldier opens the chest and finds it full of copper coins. He scatters the coins through his hands

It's true. Copper coins! More than I've ever been paid in all my years in the army ... (*He starts to fill his pouches. Pause*) But, if I can have silver ... I'd better leave room for it! (*To the Dog*) I'll just take that much, thank you.

The Dog makes another "mmmmaammmm" sound

I'll need that apron — I'm going next door.

The Dog doesn't budge, but makes a happy, friendly sound

I said I need the apron. I have to take it with me. Will you get off it please?

More happy sounds from the Dog

(*To the audience*) Hallo, hallo. She didn't give any instructions about this. (*To the Dog*) Hey! You! Off that apron!

The Dog barks a happy, booming bark. But he doesn't move off the apron. The Soldier appeals to the children

What do you say to a dog when it won't get off something? Like you get up for a second to poke the fire and right away he's in your favourite chair! What d'you say to get him off?

He gets various suggestions and tries them, but to no avail. The word we want is "Copper." If a child suggests it, we see the Dog react, sit up, take notice and howl a respectful howl. If the audience doesn't suggest the word, the Soldier says:

At this rate I shall get no silver or gold ... All I'll get is copper ...

The Dog howls. The Soldier notes the effect of the word and gets the children to say it with him

Hey — that got him. Copper!

The Dog howls again

Will you all say it? One, two, three ...

As they say it, the Dog gets off the apron, swings about and moves back to the chest

That did it. Thanks. Let's try my luck next door.

The Lights change

The Dog and chest disappear

The Soldier mimes moving back into the lamp-lit hall. As he turns the key:

The Narrators appear

The Soldier mimes moving through the second door and into the second room as the Narrators speak

Narrators (*in hushed tones, suspensefully*)
Back to the hall where the lamps were burning,
His pockets with copper coin a-jingling,
And soon the key in the lock he was turning ....
And every nerve in his body was tingling ....
As, slowly, he opened the second door ....

And there in a huge, great room he saw,
Yes you've guessed ...
The dog that guarded the silver chest!

The Dog with eyes as big as millwheels appears, guarding a silver chest

The Narrators disappear

Soldier Hey! What a dog! What a stare! You! Eyes as big as millwheels —
stop staring. It's rude, and it'll spoil your eyesight. (*To the audience*) I'll
show him the apron ...

*The Soldier spreads the apron on the ground with a flourish and a loud, deep,
hound-like howl reverberates from the dog. It shrinks back slightly. Then it
gets on the apron*

He's more afraid of it than the other. Now for the second chest ...

*He opens the chest. It is filled with silver coins. They cascade through his
fingers*

The Narrators appear

Narrators Inside the chest was a silver sea ...
And as many coins as the sea makes shells.
He weighed them with wonder, in a state of glee,
And tinged them together with a sound like bells!

The Narrators disappear

Soldier Pure silver coins! Enough to pay a whole company of soldiers. Well
it's no use keeping the copper coins. I'll make way for these! (*He tips
out the copper coins and stuffs his pouches and pockets with silver*)
Think what I can buy with this! I'll give up soldiering for good. Here
— it's heavy. I can hardly walk. Maybe I'll give the third room a miss.
(*He thinks*) But it's got gold in there ... I'll have to see it ... (*To the children
in the audience*) What's the word to get him off? (*He gets them to shout
"Silver"*)

The Dog gets off the apron and disappears, along with the chest

The Lights change

The Soldier mimes going back into the lamp-lit hall

   The Narrators appear

Narrators Again to the hall of the lanterns glowing,
           To dare the most frightening dare of the three;
           And the trembling in his hand was showing,
           As, little by little, he turned the key.

   The Narrators disappear

There is a quick Black-out

When the Lights come up, they reveal the huge, turning eyes — as big as the round towers of Copenhagen — of the third Dog beaming down on the Soldier from the heavens. (This is an effect rather than an actor dressed as a dog.) The Dog is guarding a gold chest

Soldier What a creature! The biggest eyes of all! Imagine being a thief ... and coming face to face with that! If he ran for sticks they'd be as big as tree trunks! (*To the Dog*) Good-evening. (*To the audience*) I'll stay calm and show him the apron.

He shows the Dog the apron — the resulting howl is the loudest yet. The dog shrinks back slightly

He's even more afraid of it. Here goes ...

He opens the chest. A golden light emanates

   The Narrators appear

Narrators And gold gleams danced about the room,
           As he saw what was guarded by that hound.
           Gold coins that shimmered through the gloom ...
           Oh what a treasure house he'd found!

   The Narrators disappear

Soldier Gold! This is it! Real gold! Enough to buy the whole city of Copenhagen — and all the gingerbread men — all the rocking-horses and riding-whips and tin-soldiers in the whole world! I'm sorry silver — you'll have to go and make way for the gold. (*He fills everything he's carrying with gold, tipping out the silver to make room for it. Soon he can't even stand up straight*) I'm loaded — no — I've got some room in my hat. (*He puts some more gold in his hat — he almost crawls*) I think that'll do. I feel as though I'm carrying a load of cannon balls — and the cannon! Is he going to let me take it? (*To the audience*) Say the word with me: "Gold"!

There is a huge howling sound from Dog that nearly blasts the Soldier away. He makes vain attempts to get back on his feet

I'll need the old witch to pull me. (*Calling*) Hey! Witch! Pull me up! Pull me up!

He tugs on the rope several times as the Lights change. There is a dissolve to:

SCENE 4

We see the oak tree and the Witch hauling on the rope

The Narrators appear

Narrators (*harmonizing the first word*)
Up from as deep underground as a steeple.
Up from the buried hall of light.
Up past worm and mole and beetle,
Up through the oak to the moonlit night.

The Narrators disappear

Witch Come on! Nearly there! Climb!
Soldier (*off*) Pull!

The Witch hauls, strongly and athletically

The Soldier emerges from the tree and the Witch reverts to being old and frail

Witch Don't make me do all the work. I'm only a weak and frail old woman ...

The Soldier is stuck

Soldier	Pull!
Witch	Oh my arms! Oh my back!
Soldier	Why didn't you pull quicker when I called out?
Witch	Because you've forgotten what this task was about ...
Soldier	What? I got all this gold. What did I forget?
Witch	The tinder box that you said you'd get!
Soldier	How do you know I've forgotten? Could be in here. (*He pats his pocket*)
Witch	It was Grandma's — I'd feel it if it was near.
Soldier	I can buy you a thousand with what's in my pack ...
Witch	It must be my grandma's. You'll have to go back.
Soldier	Back?
Witch	Back! (*She looks fearfully at the sky*) It's nearly dawn. I can sense the sun ... Go back and see the job properly done.
Soldier	For a tinder box? D'you think I'm a fool? Still, you're right. Mustn't break the soldier's rule: When you do a deal you see it through ...

The Soldier exits down the tree

Witch	(*suddenly witch-like again*) Bring me the tinder box or the worse for you! (*She waits by the tree*)

The Narrators appear

Narrators	While she waits for the Soldier we'll tell you What a tinder box was supposed to do. You see, matches weren't invented yet, So to light a fire or candle, you had to get Some tinder in a metal box. Tinder's anything that burns. Hay or straw. There's a wheel that sparks as it turns. The sparks light the tinder; you light your candle from the flame ...

We hear the Soldier call from below

Soldier	(*off*) Hey ... witch! Pull me up, old dame!
Witch	(*calling down to him*) Have you got it this time round?

Soldier   (*off*)
             Just pull me up from underground!

The Soldier emerges from the tree holding the tinder box. His pack,
pouches, etc. are still bulging with gold

Witch   Give it me!
Soldier   Wait! What d'you want it for?
Witch   To kindle a fire and watch the flames roar ...
Soldier   I don't believe you. You're telling lies.
             Look — I can see it in your eyes ...
             Tell the truth ...

The dawn is approaching and the Witch panics

Witch   Give it me! The night's done.
             I feel the mists of morning,
             And the world waking up all stretching and yawning ...
             Give me the tinder box — I have to go!
Soldier   Only if you tell me why you want it so ...
             All evil things are afraid of the light.
             It's just as I thought. You're a witch all right!
Witch   Give it me!
Soldier   But I went through danger. I've a right to be told.
Witch   I'll tell you nothing.
Soldier   What?
Witch   Nothing I said!
Soldier   Listen ... If you won't tell me ... (*He draws his sword*)
             I'll cut off your head.
Witch   The dawn! The sun!

There is a stream of light

Soldier   Tell me what I want to know!
Witch   I won't.
Soldier   All right then, Witch. Off you go!

He sweeps with his sword. There is a great flash of light. The Soldier is
horrified and crouches, blinded by the flash. The Witch's clothes fall in a
heap revealing a hideous, evil creature of the night

   The Witch exits, screaming

The Lights change to denote a gentle sunrise

What was *that*?? Whatever it was I sent it packing. And these can go to the dogs.

He flings her clothes offstage (except her apron, still tucked in his pack). He senses some disquiet in the audience

All right — I got rid of her. She was a witch! Look what a beautiful day it is now she's gone. Ah! Her tinder box — that can go too ... (*He is about to throw it when he changes his mind and puts it in his pack*) No, might come in useful. Hey, I can hardly carry all this gold. I'll put some in her apron — now she won't need it herself. Then off to Copenhagen to enjoy all my wealth! (*He sets off for Copenhagen, singing*)

Song: I'm Rich

I'm rich, I'm rich!
And all on account of that old witch ...
If only she'd said why,
She wouldn't have had to die ...
Still, I'm rich, I'm rich, I'm rich, I'm rich,
I'm rich, I'm rich, I'm rich!

I'm rich, I'm rich!
No more sleeping in a ditch ...
I'll sleep in silken sheets instead,
In a mile-high feather bed,
I'm rich, I'm rich ... *etc.*

I'm rich, I'm rich!
Now everything will go without a hitch;
I'll have money up to here,
I'll buy the brewery out of beer ...
I'm rich, I'm rich ... *etc.*

I'm rich, I'm rich!
I could pay someone to scratch me when I itch!
I'll have servants by the score,
I won't do nothing anymore ...
I'll have a chap to clean my boots

> And one to press my suits ...
> A bloke to comb my locks
> And a maid to wash my socks ...
> And a flunkey every day
> Just to shoo the flies away ...
>
> I'm rich, I'm rich, I'm rich, filthy rich,
> I'm rich, tiddly-ich, I'm rich!

There is a dissolve to:

SCENE 5

The Royal Palace

The King, Queen, Princess, Lady-in-waiting and Officer are discovered, all in a sad mood

The Narrators appear

Narrators In Copenhagen at the palace of the King
Neither King nor Queen were enjoying anything.
They were sad, there were angry and full of gloom,
As they summoned Princess Sigrid to the royal drawing-room.
Princess Sigrid was their only daughter ...
And so lovely that scores of princes sought her ...
Until, one day, a fortune-teller came.
He told her fortune — which caused so much pain.
He said: no prince would ever marry her. Instead,
A common soldier she would wed.

The Narrators disappear

Queen How can she marry a common soldier!
King Over my dead body!
Queen Sigrid ...
When we're gone you'll sit on the throne
And be Queen of Denmark. Better you reign alone
Than marry the lowest of the low.
King A common soldier like you see standing in a row!
Never! (*To the Officer*) Go and proclaim
That any common soldier found in Copenhagen
Will be thrown in jail ...

Officer	Yes, sire!
Queen	And then be hung!
Officer	M'am, I shall without fail.
Queen	(*to the King*)
	You should have stopped that fortune-teller
	Before he said she'd marry a lout!
King	I punished him — he was whipped and thrown out!
Lady	Oh, Majesty what a dismal fate!
Princess	Why is everyone in such a state?
	This soldier — he could be really nice ...
King	What??
Queen	You don't know common soldiers. They have fleas and lice!
Lady	Oh, ma'am. I read of a prince who didn't marry a proper
	princess ...
	It got their lives in a terrible mess.
	In the end they had an awful break-up.
	She spent all his money on hair-dos and make-up.
Queen	You see!
King	Dear daughter — you must listen to your mother and me.
	We've thought and thought about what to do.
Queen	And we only want what's best for you ...
	We want to protect you. Please don't glower!
	We simply want you to live in the Copper Tower.
Princess	The Copper Tower! A prison? Why? What have I done?
King	You can have all your comforts ...
Princess	But I'll never see the sun!
Queen	Your lady-in-waiting will be with you ...
Lady	Oh, Your Highness, I will!
King	And always remember we love you still ...
Princess	(*indicating the Officer*)
	He's going to take me there and lock me inside?
Queen	But your marriage! We can't let fate decide ...
Princess	You'll shut the gates and lock me away?
Queen	Be sensible, Sigrid ...
King	You'll thank us one day ...
Princess	One day isn't now. Oh, Father, it's unjust.
King	I'm sorry, Daughter, but go you must ...

The Princess exits

The King motions for the Lady-in-waiting to stay

You're to keep watch over her — you understand?

Lady   Yes, Your Majesty ...
Queen   And don't start taking her side. Do as we command ...
Lady   I will, Your Majesty ... Oh dear, oh dear!

She exits

King   (*to the Officer*)
             Tell the town. I want them gone.
             The gallows for common soldiers from now on.

The Officer clicks his heels, bows and exits

The King and Queen sadly embrace

There is a dissolve to:

SCENE 6

Copenhagen

Clocks strike. People are out walking. There are various street vendors and a man on a hobby horse bike. A band is playing. The Soldier enters at the edge of all this activity and passes a Beggar

Beggar Spare a copper, general ...
Soldier Spare a what?
Beggar Copper ...
Soldier Why bother with copper?

The Soldier flips him a coin

       Have one of these instead. I've known times when I've had to beg for a
       crust ...
Beggar (*amazed*) But — that's gold!
Soldier I've plenty more. Am I near to Copenhagen?
Beggar You're in it, God bless you! But you're not going to go round like
       that are you?
Soldier Like what?
Beggar Dressed as a — (*whispering nervously*) common soldier ...
Soldier What d'you mean, "common"?
Beggar Only trying to keep you out of trouble. You see word is going round
       that the King don't like common soldiers.

Soldier But I've just been fighting a war for him ...

Beggar I know — unfair isn't it? I was in the last one — or I would have been if it wasn't for my feet. I'll tell you what, since you've been so generous — you can have my coat. (*He hands it to the Soldier*) It'll cover up the uniform.

Soldier Pongs a bit.

Beggar I sweat a lot ...

Soldier It's through wearing a coat ...

Beggar Hide the hat ...

Soldier This is stupid! I'm proud to be a soldier ... (*But he does so*)

Beggar Your drum's sticking out.

Soldier So's yours!

An Officer marches on and blows a horn

Officer Silence! A Royal proclamation! To all loyal citizens of Copenhagen — Be it know that any common soldier found in the city after today will be hanged on the public gallows. God Save the King!

He exits

The Beggar slinks fearfully off

Soldier What have they got against soldiers?

But the Beggar has gone. A Rose Seller approaches

Rose Seller Lovely red roses! Sweet smelling roses!

Soldier I'll take the lot ...

Rose Seller You? You couldn't buy a dandelion!

Soldier (*flipping a coin*) Will this do?

Rose Seller I can't change that!!

Soldier Keep it. In memory of comrades killed in battle. (*He takes the biggest bunch of roses*)

The Rose Seller drifts off

A Baker with gingerbread men on a tray approaches

Baker Gingerbread men! Fresh baked gingerbread men!

Soldier I must have one of those. No ... I'll buy the lot. (*He flips a gold coin and takes the whole tray*)

Boots, who works at the Inn, passes by

Then I'll eat this one — give one to this boy ——

Boots is surprised but accepts the gingerbread gladly

— The rest I'll give back to you.

He presents the tray back to the amazed Baker

Baker Why?
Soldier So you can sell 'em again!
Baker Why?
Soldier So you can make more money ... and smile! We've seen enough misery in the war.

The Baker drifts off

(*To Boots*) Now boy ——

Boots is happily munching away at his gingerbread

— I want to stay at an inn — and I want you to tell me which is the most expensive?
Boots Why, that's the one where I work — and work hard. It's run by Mrs Pin. I'm the Boots.
Soldier You mean you clean the boots?
Boots That and everything else ...
Soldier Good. I'll need someone to polish these.
Boots You? (*He looks at the Soldier's boots with distaste*) Them?
Soldier Here's a tip in advance. (*He flips a gold coin*)
Boots (*astonished*) Hey!
Soldier   Let's go and talk to Mrs Pin ...
               Lead on, Mr Boots, to your expensive inn!

The Soldier and Boots circle the stage as there is a dissolve to:

SCENE 7

The Inn

The Soldier and Boots halt in the lobby. There, they meet the irate, stiff-backed proprietor, Mrs Pin. She is horrified by the sight of the Soldier

Mrs Pin Boots! Where have you been? (*She cuffs his ear*) Who is this vile
person? Remove him from my reception area! There's a notice on the door,
if you can read, that says: "No tramps allowed"!
Boots He ain't a tramp, Mrs Pin ...
Mrs Pin (*cuffing him again*) Get him out! I have respected gentlemen staying
at this inn — he'll offend my paying guests. Ah — here are two of them
now ...

Scoff, with napkin under his chin, and Twist, a salesman, enter

Mr Scoff! Mr Twist! I apologize, Mr Twist. I wouldn't want you disturbed
for anything — but this tramp has come in here off the streets as though he
owns the place!
Scoff Looks as though he could use a few hot dinners, Mrs Pin. Get out of
here, skinny! You put me off my food!
Twist Don't give us a hard luck story. On your way! He's a shirker. Go and
get an honest job!
Soldier (*to the audience*) Watch what happens when they find out what I've
got in my pockets! (*To Mrs Pin*) First, allow me to present these to our most
gracious landlady ... (*He bows and proffers the roses*) Second, this coat is
not my coat but one I bought from a beggar — so people wouldn't get too
excited about what they'd see underneath. (*He takes off his coat, revealing
his uniform*)
Boots Oh gawd!
Mrs Pin He's a common soldier!
Scoff He is too!
Twist What a cheat!
Mrs Pin (*cuffing Boots*) Alter that notice: "No tramps or common soldiers"!
Soldier (*to the audience*) What have they got against soldiers?
Mrs Pin Send for the constable!
Soldier (*aside*) Whatever it is, it's time to stop being one. Don't be so hasty.
Hear me out. If you want to know what I am. I'm ... rich ...
Boots That's right. He got gold! I seen it.
Mrs Pin (*cuffing him*) Don't interrupt!
Soldier Could I ask you, madam, not to cuff the boy as it brings back unhappy
memories of when I was low down the ladder myself and generally being
cuffed and beaten from pillar to post. As he says: I got gold ... I'm a rich
man! (*He flips a gold coin*) Well, last night, I was travelling in my coach
to Copenhagen when I was set upon by a roaring mob of highwaymen.
They overpowered me, robbed me and stripped me naked!
Mrs Pin Goodness!

Scoff ⎱ (*together*) Oh!
Twist ⎰

Soldier They took my coach and the money they found on me. But I'd had the presence of mind to throw a bag of gold into the bushes. So I was able to get it back after they'd gone. And there I was ——

Twist No coach ——

Scoff No food ——

Mrs Pin No clothes ——

Soldier — till a soldier came marching along the road ...

Mrs Pin A *common* soldier?

Soldier No — a very uncommon soldier. A fine fellow — very bright — very generous. Sold me his uniform and went off in his underthings ...

Scoff and Twist are a mite suspicious

Twist He sold you the lot?

Soldier Yes.

Twist And the drum?

Soldier Yes.

Scoff And this apron?

Soldier (*warily*) Yes ...

Twist I never heard of a soldier wearing a check apron.

Soldier He was a cook.

Scoff (*interested*) Was he?

Twist So why's he need a drum?

Soldier All cooks have drums. Like you'll hear them say: I'll just drum up some bacon and sausage.

A silence. The joke dies

Mrs Pin What happened to all the gold?

Soldier It's here.

He opens the pack, pouches and apron and spills gold before them. A gilded light plays about them. Mrs Pin has to be supported by Boots

Mrs Pin Oh forgive me! I've misjudged you, dear sir!

Boots I was trying to tell you ...

Twist That's what I call ready money!

Scoff You could buy a lot of hot dinners with that!

Soldier Madam, may I take your finest room?

Mrs Pin Of course! Don't think too harshly of me, sir. I try so hard to give true quality of service — but hardly anyone has the money to spend these days. You shall have everything you require ...

Soldier Well, first I shall need some respectable clothes.

They start speaking in verse

Twist Ah ... It just so happens I've got some of those ...
Twist is the name. Best dealer in town
For your silk shirts, suits, shoes, socks, dressing-gown,
Spats, hats, cravats, silver-knobbed cane,
And at such low prices it's almost insane!

Scoff And my name's Scoff. I generally advise on meals.
Now for supper: oysters, larks' brains and smoked eels,
Washed down with hot toddy and, to finish, roly-poly puddin',
With jam sauce and cream, if your appetite's a good-un!

Soldier Right ... Is there a feather mattress on the bed, Mrs Pin?

Mrs Pin Oh yes!

Soldier Put another on top ... I'm going to sink in! (*He sings*)

Song (Reprise): I'm Rich

I'm rich, I'm rich!
(*Aside*) Notice how their fingers start to itch ...
All (except Soldier) (*singing*) A thousand welcomes, sir ...
You're the sort that we prefer ...
He's rich, he's rich, he's rich, he's rich,
He's rich, tiddly-itch, he's rich!

They all exit dancing as there is a dissolve to:

SCENE 8

On the way to the Copper Tower

The Narrators appear

Narrators At that very moment across the city,
You'd see a sight that would fill you with pity.
For this was the minute and this the hour
When the Princess was taken to the Copper Tower.

The Officer enters with the Princess, leading her around the stage, followed by the Lady-in-waiting carrying bags and boxes

They come to a copper gate which the Officer unlocks. They pass through and the Officer locks the gate behind him

Princess Are we there?
Officer One more gate, Your Highness ...

They pass through another gate

Princess And when will you come again to set me free?
Officer I don't know, Your Highness. It's not up to me.

He indicates the way forward and the little procession moves sadly on as there is a dissolve to:

SCENE 9

The Inn

The Soldier is asleep in a splendid four poster bed

Mrs Pin and Scoff enter, with a breakfast trolley groaning with food

Mrs Pin Good-morning! What a splendid day!
Scoff A splendid day for eating your fill. I've brought your breakfast ...
Soldier Breakfast?? What's the time?
Mrs Pin Nearly noon. Must get up soon!
Scoff Otherwise breakfast will run into lunch — unless you want your lunch first and breakfast after — but that would make tea so late you'd never have dinner and that wouldn't do at all!

Boots enters with new boots and new clothes

Boots Morning, sir! Six pairs of new boots — I'll never stop polishin'...
Mrs Pin We got the boot-maker to open up early this morning and he was able to match your size ...
Soldier Good! And new clothes ...
Mrs Pin The tailor measured you in your sleep and ran them up in the night.
Boots (*aside*) For a price!
Mrs Pin What's that?
Boots (*indicating the clothes*) Very nice!

24   The Tinder Box

Scoff wheels the trolley to the bed

Soldier Something smells good there ... What's for breakfast?
Scoff We start with a really stiff, sticky porridge, running with melted butter, cream and golden treacle. Succulent juicy kippers with pepper and lemon. Scorching hot devilled kidneys with mustard. Two lamb chops with the fat crisply done. Tender rump steak with onions on top ... Rashers of Danish bacon. Four fried eggs. Black pudding with a pinch of herbs. Plump plum tomatoes. Fresh-picked mushrooms. Deep-fried potatoes. Toast. Flapjacks. Waffles. Pancakes. Marmalade. Honey ... and strawberry jam! (*Pause*) And some pork scratchings.
Soldier Pork scratchings?
Scoff In case you get hungry afterwards. If you're not eating all the steak I'll just have a slice. (*He helps himself*)

Twist enters

Twist Good-morning — how I admire a gentleman with real style. Your new carriage has just arrived ...
Soldier (*to Twist*) My new carriage! You got that double quick, Mr Twist ——
Twist Oh when Twist says he'll do it, it's done, squire! From the finest coachmaker in Copenhagen. He happened to have one ready. Real leather upholstery and wind-down windows. And an absolute bargain!
Soldier So ... where shall I go then?
Mrs Pin The parks ——
Twist The harbour ——
Boots The pleasure gardens ——
Scoff The restaurants ——
Soldier I was thinking about the palace ...

They all look a little uncomfortable

Mrs Pin I'm not sure that would be a good idea at the moment ...
Twist No — I'd give that a miss, old son. By the way, if you've got that soldier's uniform around here somewhere we'll get rid of it for you.
Soldier No. I've got it tucked away and that's where it will stay. That soldier was a good friend to me and when I meet him I shall give him his clothes back. Come on! Out with it. What is all this about soldiers?
Mrs Pin Common soldiers ...
Soldier Why are they hanging them?
Mrs Pin You must be the only person in the city who doesn't know. The King and Queen — very unwisely in my opinion — allowed a fortune-teller to

come to the palace and he has foretold that Princess Sigrid will not marry
a prince, but a common soldier. Now I'm not snobbish, but all the same ...

Twist A very bad deal, Mrs P.

Scoff You just couldn't swallow it.

Boots (*disgusted*) Streuth! "Not snobbish"!

Twist The latest thing is that they've locked the Princess away in the Copper
Tower — surrounded by walls and a moat ——

Soldier (*getting excited*) I'd like to see her ...

Mrs Pin They won't allow anyone to see her.

Soldier What's she like?

Mrs Pin A little headstrong ——

Twist Simple tastes. Needs to spend more ——

Scoff Needs feeding up ——

Boots She's wonderful!

Soldier What if I put my best things on and rode up in my new carriage?

All No ...

Twist They might think you were a common soldier in disguise ——

Soldier Might they?

Twist — whereas you're nothing of the sort, squire. Are you?

Soldier No. Oh well. I'll just have to do what I was going to do in the first
place ...

Mrs Pin What?

Soldier Spend! (*He takes the big cash box from under the bed*)

There is a dissolve to:

SCENE 10

The Copper Tower

The Princess sits sadly in a copper chair, her Lady-in-waiting attending

The Narrators appear

Narrators In the Copper Tower, so sad to tell,
           The Princess like a prisoner in a cell,
           With a grief that she can hardly bear,
           Counts the passing days since she came there ...

The Narrators disappear

Princess What's going to happen. Is this to be my fate?

> Do they want me here till I'm a hundred and eight?
> I want to go through the streets as I used to do,
> Talk to the people and say: "How are you?"
> Reach out to poor children and touch their hands
> And ease some of the suffering in these lands.

Lady   We must do what we can to drive the sulks away!
             There's needlework ——

She hands the Princess a drum shaped needlework box, then a home loom and knitting

> — knitting, your home loom set — just say.
> Or pottery! You were always so good at throwing.

Princess All I want to be good at is getting up and going.
              Copper chair, copper walls, copper bed too ...
Lady   But copper's good for rheumatics ...
Princess I don't have them ...
Lady   I do!

A silence. The Princess finds she has picked up some big knitting needles. She begins to tap a faint drum beat on the needlework box. The Lady-in-waiting is nervous

> What are you thinking?
Princess About the soldier ...
Lady   Put him out of your mind!
Princess But why shouldn't he be pleasant, generous and kind?
Lady   Please don't! Such talk would make your mother grieve.
              For all you know he wipes his nose on his sleeve.
Princess I'll embroider him hankies. I'll say, "Use these, please".
Lady   But his manners! He might use a knife to eat peas!

The Princess gazes from the window and drums, a rat-tat-tat

Princess I see him marching along with his drum ...
Lady   Where?
Princess In my mind.
Lady   Oh thank goodness! I thought that he'd come!
Princess I see him strong ... cheerful ... a bit rough ... but funny.
Lady   What? Eating peas off his knife with his nose all runny?
Princess Don't be so petty. He'll learn how to behave.
              It's in the heart where it counts. Is he honest and brave?

> I think, if I don't meet him it could spell my doom.
> I'll take my life — not grow old in this dark, copper tomb.

Lady   Oh Lord! You'll make me as sad as you ...

Princess   I'm sorry. Have a sleep. I'm so selfish — it's true ...
> I'll watch from my window. This mood will pass.
> And I promise I'll wake you if he knocks on the glass!

The Lady-in-waiting is nervous for a moment then smiles at being teased

Lady   A sweet good-night, Your Highness. Sleep well.

Princess   Good-night.

The Lady-in-waiting exits

> How can I sleep in a prison cell?

She sits for a moment, still tapping the drum-beat on the needlework box. She starts to sing

Song: Where are you?

> Where are you
> My common soldier?
> As you march
> To drum and fife.
> Will I take you
> For my husband?
> Will you take me
> For your wife?
>
> Oh where are you?
> Where are you?
> Oh where
> My love
> My life?

There is a dissolve to:

SCENE 11

The Pleasure Gardens

The Chorus are dancing a polka. Champagne is being poured. Lanterns hang in the trees. It is nearing Christmas and there is a silvery, snowy feeling in the air. A Croupier sets up a wheel of fortune. The Soldier joins in the dance, with his money box still under his arm

Soldier	More champagne! A toast. To happy days!
All	Happy days!
Soldier	And remember — I'm the one who pays ...
	Now — what's next? Another dance? (*He notices the wheel of fortune*)
	What's this?
Croupier	The wheel of fortune — take your chance!
Soldier	The wheel of fortune?
Croupier	That's the one! Feel like a flutter?
Soldier	Why not?
Croupier	You're on! Put money on any number you choose. If it comes up you win double ...
Soldier	And if it don't?
Croupier	You lose.
Soldier	Well I can't think of a number out of the blue ... Ah! The legs of a centipede! (*Calling*) Thirty-two!

The Soldier puts some money down. The wheel rattles round, slows and stops

Croupier	Sorry, sir. One hundred! Wheel of fortune!
Soldier	Why didn't I say a hundred? Lost so soon? All right! (*He puts even more money down*) One hundred!

The wheel clicks round and stops

Croupier	Thirty-two!
Soldier	What?
Croupier	Again, sir? I'm sure you'll win ...
Soldier	No — here's a tip — my luck's not in.

A one-legged Beggar approaches the Soldier

Beggar	Spare a copper for a man with one leg ...

Soldier	D'you lose it in the war?
Beggar	Yessir!
Soldier	And you have to beg!

He gives the one-legged Beggar a coin

Beggar   May you have your heart's desire ... You're too good.

The one-legged Beggar leaves

Soldier   My heart's desire. I wish I could ...

*There is the tap-tap-tap of a stick as a poor widow comes up to the Soldier —
he thinks it's the Witch*

	Whassat?
Widow	Pity me, sir ... a poor, widowed mother, tired and sick ...
Soldier	I thought you were someone else, tapping with your stick.
Widow	Be generous, sir. I've four children to feed.
Soldier	Here. I've seen many a father lost — you mustn't be in need.
Widow	God bless you, sir!
Soldier	As I hope he will.
	More champagne for my friends. The night's young still! (*He sways, hugging the cash box*)

Scoff and Twist enter. Scoff has champagne

Twist	Ah — here he is! (*Aside*) The worse for wear ...
Scoff	A drop o' fizz? (*Aside*) He's in need of repair ...
Soldier	I'm hungry ... I'm starving ... I must eat soon.

A sign with "Blue Moon" written on it appears as there is a dissolve to:

SCENE 12

A Nightclub

A Waiter puts out tables and chairs

Twist   Then let's get a table at the old *Blue Moon* ...

The Waiter shows them to a table

Soldier   I thought I was a soldier begging in the street ...

Scoff and Twist laugh heartily

Scoff   But you're not ... are you?
Twist   You're here for a treat.
                (*Aside*) A soldier? What's he saying?
Scoff   We'll order some food. (*Aside*) As long as he's paying.
                Waiter! The three course special with the cold roast pheasant ...
Waiter   Right away, sir!

The Waiter exits

The Soldier shakes the money box

Soldier   Just a moment. Here's something unpleasant ... (*He opens the
                box and turns it upside down*)
                The box is empty!
Twist   Oh, squire ... (*Aside*) I smell an unhappy ending ...
Scoff   You mean the gold's all gone?
                (*Aside*) Well, he has been spending.
Soldier   Not a sliver.
                But I could borrow some.
                I've been a good giver ...

Twist and Scoff get the idea and slowly rise

Twist   Well, never mind. I'm not feeling too bright.
Scoff   And I was thinking of getting an early night.

As they move away, they speak to each other confidentially

Scoff   Borrow off me? I eat all I earn.
Twist   I need mine for business. I've no money to burn.

The Waiter enters with food

Waiter   Here you are, sir!
                Turtle soup, tender succulent pheasant in cranberry sauce ...
                And a chocolate *bombe surprise* for the final course!
Twist   (*aside to the Waiter*)
                He's got no money!

The Waiter takes the food away

Scoff and Twist exit

Soldier	Bring that back! You've got to serve me ...
	I'll find money tomorrow. Tonight serve me free!
Waiter	Sorry, sir. You'll have to pay.
Soldier	But ...
Waiter	If you don't mind, sir — the cabaret.

The Cabaret Singer — a lady swathed in ostrich feathers and black lace, with, perhaps, a slight German accent — enters. As many of the company as possible enter to sit at the tables and listen. The Cabaret Singer sings, slowly and smokily

Song: Let's See Your Money First

Cabaret Singer   You can have the prettiest dolly in the window.
                     You can have the nicest sweeties from the shelf.
                     And all those lovely things upon the counter,
                     You can have them wrapped and keep them for yourself.
                     You can go to town to all the finest restaurants,
                     And eat the tastiest dishes till you burst ...
                     But just before you do,
                     Someone's going to say to you ...
                     Let's see your money first.

                     Let's see your money ...
                     Let's see your money, honey
                     Let's see your money first!

The tempo quickens as the Company sing the chorus and engage in a wild dance. During this the Soldier tries to get at the food but it is whipped away from him by the Waiter

Chorus   Let's see your money ...
                     Let's see your money, honey
                     Let's see your money first!

The tempo slows

Cabaret Singer   You can go and see the greatest entertainers,
With songs and jokes and tricks for your delight.
You can ride in your own carriage to the theatre;
And to a ball where you can dance all night.
You can have the clothes you always saw yourself in ...
So you, thank God, will never look your worst.
But whatever you wish, my dear
Someone'll whisper in your ear:
Let's see your money first.

Let's see your money ...
Let's see your money, sonny
Let's see your money first!

The Company sing and dance, faster and faster, in a great whirling, money-grabbing chorus, mocking the Soldier with his empty cash box

Chorus   Let's see your money ...
Let's see your money, sonny
Let's see your money first! *etc.*

The Soldier is pushed and shoved and turned about as he runs from them

He is thrown out of the club

The Company continue revelling and singing in triumph as there is a dissolve to:

S<small>CENE</small> 13

The Attic of the Inn

It is bare and cold. The Soldier is asleep on the floor under a dirty, ragged blanket. He wears his long johns. His old army uniform is bundled in a corner with his sword, drum and pack, etc. He moans and cries out. He is still in the "nightmare" of the previous scene

The Narrators appear

Narrators When the Soldier got himself back to the inn
He was thrown out of his room by Mrs Pin.

> He'd got no money — so no feather bed.
> On the floorboards, in the attic, he had to sleep instead.

The Narrators disappear

The Soldier suddenly wakes

Soldier Where am I? Oh, up in the loft. Thrown out of the best room, with one measly blanket, on the bare floor ...

Boots enters with the Soldier's old boots

Boots Hallo! I've brought your old boots.

Soldier But they're dirty ...

Boots Landlady said because you hadn't paid I had to put the dirt back on. The coachmakers have just taken away your coach. It wasn't paid for.

Soldier But I gave Twist the money ...

Boots He ain't called Twist for nothing. She's also sold your posh clothes to pay for all the dozens of meals you had last week.

Soldier That wasn't me, that was Scoff! Look, they're friends ... I'll sort it out with them. Ask them to come up and see me.

Boots I did. They said there was too many stairs to climb. Landlady wants you out—now. But I can say you've gone. She won't come up here. Hasn't got the puff. Then you can lie low for a while. And soon you'll be all right—I mean—you're a rich man really, ain't you? Won't be long before you've got money again, will it?

Soldier Er ... no. But I've none now and I'm starving.

Boots She says you wasn't to have no food.

Soldier I'll give you something in exchange ...

Boots Well — I wouldn't mind that old drum there ...

Soldier No — the drum keeps me company. Here. Have the sword.

Boots But they'll know it came from a soldier. I'll be arrested.

Soldier Then don't — it brought me enough bad luck. All I want now is something to eat. Anything!

Boots I tell you what. I'll see what there is in the dustbins.

Boots exits

The Soldier puts on his uniform

Soldier I'll have to wear my uniform again. That means I can't go out. I need cheering up. My drum. Always cheers you up, tapping a drum. (*To the*

audience) Anyone like a tap? Tell you what — whoever has the cleanest
boots can have a tap. (*He moves around the audience looking for the child
with the cleanest shoes*) Yours aren't bad. One tap. (*To someone else*) You
can have two taps ... (*He finds a pair that dazzle him totally*) Go on. Tap
away!

We hear Mrs Pin off, as though she is calling up to the attic

Mrs Pin (*off*) Will you make less noise. Less noise! If you're not gone soon
I'll have you thrown out!
Soldier Sshh! I'll tap quietly. Sshh! Takes my mind off my stomach. (*He taps
very quietly, a steady beat*) Maybe the Princess will hear it in her tower.
She's a prisoner like me. She needs cheering up.

As he taps the Copper Tower appears

We see the Princess inside the tower

The Narrators appear

Narrators   In the Copper Tower, all forlorn,
                 The Princess sits waiting, night and morn,
                 And wishing she had never been born.

The Narrators disappear

Princess My lady-in-waiting is asleep again. She's as bored with this tower
as I am. I'll do some drumming, very quietly so's not to wake her. Maybe
my soldier might hear it ...

She begins to tap in rhythm with the Soldier. Then she sings

Song: Where Are You? (Reprise)

           Where are you?
           My common soldier?
           As you march
           To drum and fife.
           Will I have you
           For my husband?
           Will you have me

        For your wife?

The Soldier joins in

Soldier ⎫
Princess ⎰
        Oh where are you?
        Where are you?
        Oh where
        My love
        My life?

The Soldier sings his verse, with the Princess singing in counterpoint

        Where are you
        Princess of sadness?
        Prisoner in
        Your tower so high ...

        What I'd do
        To gain your freedom
        More than all
        My gold would buy.

        Where are you?
        Where are you?
        My true
        Love here
        Am I.

They sing together, though they are far apart

        Where are you
        My star of fortune?
        Where are you
        My hope so bright?
        Will a happy ever after
        Bring an end
        To this dark night?

        Oh where are you?
        Where are you?
        Oh where

My love
My light?

As the Lights fade we hear their quiet tapping in unison. Then silence

Black-out

ACT II

The Attic of the Inn

The Soldier sleeps under his blanket

The Narrators creep in

Narrators The Soldier, now without his gold,
Is forced to sleep in the freezing loft,
As November turns to December cold,
He dreams of the featherbed so soft.
Sometimes, at a sliding fall of snow,
On the slates above him, he opens his eyes ...
Hears sounds of laughter from below ——

There is the sound of laughter from "below"

—— And smells roast beef and apple pies ...

At the sound of the laughter the Soldier sits up, sniffing

The Narrators disappear

Soldier They're all feeding their faces down there in the dining-room and I get nothing. I haven't had a crust for days. And it's freezing — but Mrs Pin won't give me anything else to cover myself ...

He huddles in his blanket and begins to sing the following: a gloomy, tuneless, over-and-over kind of song:

> One blanket for my be-ed ...
> One blanket for my be-ed ...
> One blanket for my be-ed ...
> One blanket, *etc.*

He notices the children in the audience

(*Speaking*) You could sing that. Mind you, you have to feel really gloomy. I mean really. Feel gloomy then. I want to see some real long faces. Right. The words are: "One blanket for my be-ed ... "

He conducts them gloomily through the gloomy song

> (*Singing*) One blanket for my be-ed ...
> One blanket for my be-ed, *etc.*

Accidentally, the Soldier's finger goes through a hole in the blanket. It gives him an idea for developing the song. He gets the children to sing along with him:

> One blanket with a hole in it for my be-ed ...
> One blanket with a hole in it for my be-ed, *etc.*

He sniffs at the blanket and has a further idea. He gets the children to sing along:

> One smelly blanket with a hole in it for my be-ed ...
> One smelly blanket with a hole in it for my be-ed, *etc.*

He brings the song to a close. When the audience is settled and thinks the singing is over, he sniffs at the blanket again

(*Speaking*) Smells as though the cat's been sick on it.

He thinks, then re-commences the gloomy song:

> (*Singing*) One smelly blanket that the cat's been sick on
> With a hole in it for my be-ed, *etc.*

In the middle of this, Boots arrives with various things stuffed under his jacket. He unwraps layers and layers of crumpled paper

Boots (*speaking*) Sh! Sh! She's getting suspicious. If she hears anything she'll throw you out. Now ... I got you half a fish pie out of the bin — nearly walked out. Some cheese that got trod on in the dining-room — I've dusted it — and a chunk of last week's mouldy ol' bread they was going to throw to the birds.

Soldier I'm doing all right, aren't I?
Boots Ain't finished. Water — out of the cat's bowl but he'd hardly touched it — and a needle ...

Boots gives the Soldier the water (in a bottle), produces a needle and reaches for the Soldier's boots

Soldier What's that?
Boots A leather needle to mend your boots.
Soldier I'll do it!
Boots You been a rich man. You ain't ever mended boots!
Soldier Listen — I'll tell you the truth, 'cos I trust you. I'm a common soldier ——
Boots Thought so ——
Soldier — and proud of it. You won't give me away?

Boots gives him a withering look as he starts speaking in verse

Boots   I once knew a kid
               Kept a skylark in a cage.
               You know what I did?
               I was in such a rage ...
               I let it out — heard it sing ...
               Up there — the skylark — risen!
               If I done that for a bird,
               Would I put a man in prison?

There is the very faint sound of a lark

Boots exits

Soldier A good lad. Well, I'm mending the boots. I got my way. Here — can't see in here. What a dark and dingy day. I had a stub of candle somewhere. That'll put us right. No — even if I had it I can't get it to light. Ah! I know where it is. You guessed it, boys an' gels? Where would you put a candle end? In the tinder box — what else? (*He is delighted, then abashed*) But where did I put *that*? Let's see what we got ... (*He starts to take things out of his hat, pouches and pack*) Bit of rope ... Pipe ... Tobacco. Fish hooks. My liquorice root ... Nope! Broken compass. Spare long johns, a pair of worn-out socks ... (*He glances at the audience*) And here it is! The tinder box! (*He opens it and looks doubtful*) Here's the candle end but the tinder looks damp. There's a rhyme for making a tinder box light — now what was it? Yes ...

> One and two ...
> Two and three ...
> Tinder box, tinder box,
> Spark for me.

He looks at the tinder box expectantly. Nothing happens

Oh, of course! I have to strike it!

He strikes it. Instantly, there is a flash of sparks from the tinder box. A great doggy breathing, panting sound, getting louder and louder, is heard

> *The Dog with eyes as big as saucers bounds on and comes to a halt in front of the Soldier*

What a surprise! Old saucer eyes!
Dog What is your wish, my master?
Soldier He speaks! You mean I can have anything?
Dog Yes, master!
Soldier Money?
Dog Yes, master!

The Dog makes a musical howl and a bag of copper coins appears

Soldier Copper coins! Now I see why the old witch wanted this tinder box ...
  If I strike it twice do I get silver?
Dog Yes, master!
Soldier (*to the audience*) Do the rhyme again. With me:
> One and two ...
> Two and three ...
> Tinder box, tinder box,
> Spark for me!
> One! Two!

He strikes the tinder box twice. There are more sparks and flashes and a deep dog howl as:

The Dog with eyes as big as millwheels arrives. A bag of silver appears

And if I strike it three times ... ? *(To the audience)* Again!
     One and two ...
     Two and three ...
     Tinder box, tinder box,
     Spark for me!
     One! Two! Three!

He strikes the tinder box three times and there is a deeper howl still as:

The Dog with eyes like the round towers of Copenhagen arrives (stage effect). A bag of gold appears

Gold! And whenever I want more I just strike the tinder box?
Three Dogs *(together)* Yes, master!

There is great howling and barking as the three Dogs slowly disappear

The Soldier is rooted to the spot as, at first, he's a bit disturbed by his sudden reversal of fortune. He speaks the words of the song harshly

Song: I'm Rich (Reprise)

Soldier   I'm rich. I'm rich.
              I'll never have to give my boots a stitch.
              Now I can have money when I like ...
              With the tinder box to strike

He picks up his gear and uniform and moves off

              I'm rich, I'm rich, I'm rich, I'm rich,
              I'm rich, I'm rich, I'm rich ...

He exits, still speaking the words, as there is a dissolve to:

SCENE 2

The Inn

Scoff and Twist wheel on the four poster bed. Scoff, Twist, Mrs Pin, Boots and the Narrators burst into the song in a manic, upbeat style

Song (cont.): I'm Rich (Reprise)

Mrs Pin ⎫	
Scoff ⎪	He's rich! He's rich!
Twist ⎬	It's good to see him back on his old pitch.
Boots ⎪	Out of that dark den,
Narrators ⎭	In his feather bed again

Mrs Pin   I never wanted him to go,
He has such taste and style, you know!
We'll have a spend that never ends,
And he won't forget his friends ...

They dance around the bed as they sing the chorus

> He's rich
> He's rich, *etc.*

The Soldier enters, wearing his uniform. He carries the tattered blanket

Twist   (*speaking*) Ah here he is!
Mrs Pin Naughty man! You've got that old uniform on!
Soldier What d'you expect? My other clothes have gone ...
Mrs Pin (*guiltily*)
          Ah ... yes ...
Twist   (*fast*)
          Well done!
          I always said a man like you
          Would have a way of pulling through ...
Mrs Pin Oh I always believed you'd find your feet!
Boots   After she'd thrown you in the street ...
Mrs Pin What?? What did you say?

She almost cuffs him but stops herself and smiles a sickly smile

          Ha, ha, ha ... he's being a tease. Off to supper!
All   Hurray!
Soldier Not for me. I shall take my ease.
Twist   But aren't we going on the town?
Soldier With my feather bed back? I'm going to lie down.
          I'm a little bit stiff and a trifle sore ...
          I think it's through sleeping on the floor.

They all look a little guilty

Mrs Pin   I'll get you some supper. You must eat your fill.
             And don't hesitate, if there's anything you lack.
Soldier   I won't. By the way — (*He hands her the tattered blanket*)
             You can have this back.

Mrs Pin takes it in utter fury and embarrassment, then exits

Scoff and Twist realize it's no use persisting with the Soldier and creep away after her

Boots pauses before following

Boots   Well done, Soldier ...

He exits

Soldier Well he said it. I am a soldier. A common soldier. I don't want to go on with this rich-man guise any more.

He lies back on the pillows of the four poster to think. The Narrators move in

Narrators Now he thinks of the Princess Sigrid
             Locked behind the copper gate.
             Tries in his mind to see her clearly ...
Soldier   I can't! I can't! Though I want to dearly!
Narrators Thinks what a waste of all her beauty ...
             Thinks it is a soldier's duty
             To free her from her fate ...
Soldier   Yes! But how?
Narrators How to break those cruel locks ...

The Soldier sits up

Soldier   The tinder box!

He gets the tinder box and speaks to the children

             Saucer eyes ... Could he bring her? ... Bring her to me?

Bring her from that copper cell?
Whisper, whisper, whisper children ...
Whisper with me now the spell.
(*Softly and quietly, with the children*)
One and two ...
Two and three,
Tinder box, tinder box,
Spark for me ...

He strikes once. The tinder box sparks and we hear the great cosmic dog panting as before

The Dog with eyes as big as saucers enters, eyes rolling

Dog   Master! What is your wish at this late hour?
Soldier   Bring me the Princess from her tower.
                I know it's late. She may be asleep ...
                But I must see her ...
                Even for one minute — or I think I shall weep!
                Can you?
Dog   Yes, master — easily.
Soldier   Go through doors without a key?
Dog   Yes, master — leave it all to me.

The Dog pads off

Soldier   (*aghast at what he has done*)
                No, no! Come back. I'm not quite ready!
                My face is on fire. I'm starting to sweat!
                I'll stand to attention to hold me steady.
                Was that him? Is he coming back?

The Lights grow, anticipating her arrival. The Soldier stares straight ahead, stiffly at attention and fearful

Narrators   Through the pearly pools of moonlight,
                Silvered in the frosty air;
                Diamond dust of distant star bright
                Touches the sleepy half-closed eyelids
                Of the Princess Sigrid fair ...
                Hardly waking on the Dog's back,
                Through silent city came she there.

The Dog enters with the Princess on his back

They are a beautiful vision under the night sky as they move slowly round the stage. The Princess is lost in sleep, but now and then her eyes open as though she is dreaming, on the edge of waking. The Soldier doesn't dare look at her when the Dog stops by him. But he eventually musters his courage

Soldier Common soldier, Your Highness ...
Dog   She sleeps. She will not wake.
Soldier Fine. Yes. Well. What course do I take?
             To say I've never seen beauty would not be true.
             I've seen girls in every country I've marched through.
             In Denmark's land and high Germany,
             And in Holland's tulip fields, girls smiled at me.
             But never by lake or forest pine
             Have I seen such a single beauty shine.
             What a stupid fortune-teller
             To say she could be mine!

The Dog moves as if to go

             Where are you going?
Dog   You said only for a minute, master.
Soldier Did I? Compared with mine your minute's faster.

He stares at the Princess. She moans and stirs. He stands to attention

             Common soldier, Your Highness.
             Not sure what to do.
             But soldiers kiss girls.
             So I'll kiss you.

He kisses her. There is a magical humming sound. She opens her eyes and looks at him without "seeing". She smiles, then closes her eyes

The Dog bears her slowly away

The Soldier salutes, sadly. He is left, hopelessly in love, as Lights fade to black

SCENE 3

The Copper Tower

The King and Queen are visiting. The Lady-in-waiting greets them in a state of agitation

Lady	Your Majesties! Your Majesties!
	The Princess! The Princess!
King	Has she got out?
Lady	No ...
Queen	Is she in distress?
Lady	No ...
King	What then?
Lady	Last night she was her usual self — sad and rather tearful —
	And what d'you think's happened now?
Queen	What?
Lady	She's got up feeling cheerful!
Queen	Oh dear ...
Lady	I distinctly heard her singing in her morning bath.
	And once — just once — I swear I heard her laugh!
	And she's eating *all* her breakfast and asking for more.
King	What's the meaning of this?
Queen	We'd better explore.

The Princess enters, avidly eating thick toast

Princess	Hallo, parents! Have some tea.
	Have some toast. Have some kedgeree.
	Would you like your eggs boiled, scrambled or fried?
	They're all so delicious, it's hard to decide!
	And doesn't this weather take some beating?
King	It's cold and dismal and appears to be sleeting ...
Princess	Oh but the sky — such a lovely dark grey!
Queen	My dear, I'm your mother — have you something to say?
Princess	Erm — no.
	Well — I did have this dream where I got carried away.
King	How?
Princess	On a dog! A dog with eyes as big as this ...
Queen	Where did he carry you to?
Princess	A soldier — yes! And he gave me a kiss.
Queen	What a nice story ... *(She grits her teeth)*

King	Would you recognize this soldier?
Princess	(*warily*)
	Oh no. He was just a dream — and all dreams fade.
	Hmmm. I could use some more marmalade ...

She exits briskly with a smile

King	I have a feeling this dream wasn't a dream.
Queen	Now, now. Let's stay calm — do nothing extreme.
Lady	It must have been a dream because, you see ...
	If it wasn't she'd have woken. Like the Princess and the Pea.
King	What?
Lady	The Princess and the Pea. That Princess who couldn't sleep,
	Because someone put a single pea under her mattresses.
	And they were piled more than twenty deep!
Queen	That is a fairy story. And I don't see the relevance.
	Sigrid would sleep through a stampede of elephants.
King	She said a soldier! No doubt the one she's in danger of being
	married to ...
Queen	(*to the Lady-in-waiting*)
	Watch her properly tonight. If she's "carried away" find out
	where she's been carried to!
Lady	Your Majesty! What a clever idea!

The King and Queen exit, exasperated

The Lady-in-Waiting becomes her more uncertain self

I love the Princess — but I must obey. Oh dear! Oh dear!

The Lights fade

SCENE 4

The entrance to the Inn. Night

The Soldier comes to the door, waiting anxiously

The Narrators appear

Narrators	The Soldier sent for the Princess once more,
	And she came through the night to the old inn door.

Once more, once more, he would see her sweet face.

The Dog enters with the Princess on his back as before

The Dog came swiftly — but someone kept pace

We see the Lady-in-waiting, in coat and large walking-boots, striding short-sightedly in pursuit. She hides furtively as:

The Dog, the Princess and the Soldier exit into the inn

Lady   (*as she goes*)
                  Oh dear ... Oh dear ...
Narrators In her best walking-boots she could keep them in view.
                  They went inside ...
Lady   Oh — now what do I do? (*She looks about her*)
                  All these houses look the same and I'm terrible at getting myself
                       lost.
                  I know! I'll, mark the door so I can lead the King and Queen
                       straight to it ... (*She finds chalk in her pocket*)
                  My dressmaker's chalk. A cross by the door should do it. (*She
                       chalks a cross by the door*)
                  You see! The Queen isn't the only one that's clever.
                  The King will be pleased. They'll be grateful for ever!
                  That cross will lead right to the Princess ...
                  We'll rescue her from that soldier and make him confess.
                  (*Her air of bravado is spoiled when she suddenly realizes she
                       doesn't know the way back*)
                  Oh dear ...

She finds her way and exits

As the Lady-in-waiting goes the Dog puts his head out of the inn door and looks at the cross. his eyes rolling

Narrators Out came the Dog!
                  With his big eyes he saw
                  The cross she'd put
                  And he knew what it was for.
                  He conjures up a piece of chalk ...
                  And a doggy smile he smiles ...

The Dog makes a happy sound

> Then he goes round chalking crosses
> By every door for miles!

The Narrators disappear

The Dog carefully draws a cross by one house doorway, then another, then another, then another

Dog   My master, have no fear.
             With one cross there, another here,
             By the power of my magic paws,
             They'll never know which door is yours!

With a satisfied howl he exits to make more crosses on the doors across the city

Music. Light grows from the inn door

The Soldier and Princess emerge and kiss. The Soldier becomes clumsy and formal

Soldier   Thank you, Your Highness.
Princess   Why "Your Highness"? Why not Sigrid? I don't understand ...
Soldier   It's just that I'm so common and you're so grand.
Princess   So grand I'm in prison because of this ...
Soldier   I'd get worse than prison just for that kiss.
                 Where's Saucer Eyes?
Princess   Didn't I hear him howl?
Soldier   Dogs will be dogs. He must be on the prowl.
Princess   Maybe he thinks I should walk home this time ...
Soldier   Your Highness!
Princess   Sigrid ...
Soldier   I wish you — your — Look, d'you mind if I don't rhyme?
I wish ... Oh God! I mustn't send for you again.
Princess Why not?
Soldier Because I can never be a Prince!
Princess All right. I'll stop being a Princess ...
Soldier You can't!
Princess Don't give me orders, you common soldier! Soldiers have girlfriends. A soldier walking out with his girl. That's what I'll be. Your girl. As for palaces — why not a house? (*She starts speaking in verse*)

Not too big, not too small,
With a view of the sea and the harbour wall. (*She sings*)

Song: Copenhagen Garden

In Copenhagen,
There is a garden,
Where you can watch the ships go by
And woodlands all about,
Where children laugh and shout,
Under a bright blue sky.

In Copenhagen,
In that garden,
We'll make our own sweet world.
And no more will I be
Princess or Royalty ...
Your Copenhagen girl!

Soldier }
Princess }   In Copenhagen,
In that garden,
We'll make our own secret world
And no more will I be/No Prince could ever be
Princess or Royalty/A happy man like me
Your Copenhagen girl/With my Copenhagen girl.

As the song ends the Dog appears and waits for the Princess. She kisses the Soldier once more and, as the Lights begin to fade, exits with the Dog

Dissolve to:

SCENE 5

The same. Dawn, some minutes later

The King, Queen and Officer are led on furtively by the Lady-in-waiting. She peers about uncertainly

Queen   (*speaking*) Where is it?
King   Where's the door?
Queen   Which one? Which one?

King	What are you dithering for?
Lady	I made a cross — but I did it in the dark.
	And now — oh dear — I can't see the mark.
King	Find it! I want that soldier dangling on a rope.
	Well, we may give him a trial but he hasn't a hope.
Lady	Oh thank goodness — I've found it. This is the one ...
King	Officer — arrest him and let's be gone.
Officer	*(banging on the door)*
	Open up, open up — or we'll break your door down! *(He bangs at the door)*

A man, the Vicar, in a night-shirt and night-cap, enters from the door

Vicar	What d'you want? It's early. I'm in my night-gown.
Officer	You're arrested in the name of the King!
Vicar	Why? I haven't done anything ...
Officer	I want you out of here now! If not quicker!
Vicar	Why?
Officer	You're the common soldier ...
Vicar	I'm not, I'm the vicar ...
Officer	The vicar!
Vicar	This is the vicarage of St Swithun ...
Officer	Sorry, Your Reverence ...
Vicar	Never mind, you're forgiven.
King	Knock on that door! There's a cross there!

The King's fury drives the Officer and Lady into rapid knocking on two other doors

Two Women appear in night attire. One of them is in hysterics

1st Woman Help! It's thieves! Thieves! Get away! Get away! Call the constables. Set the dog on 'em!

2nd Woman Is that the postman? Wait a minute! Is that the post? I'm half-dressed!

Vicar How dare you disturb these good people! Be off!

Everybody shouts at once, until the King's voice booms over them all

King	Quiet!
Queen	Don't shout.
King	Away!

The Vicar and the two Women exit

	I think there's something we must find out.
	Why is there a cross on the florist and one on the baker's?
	There's even one on the undertaker's.
	In fact when you look up and down ...
	There could be a cross by every door in town!
Queen	Then we can't find him. We've drawn a blank.
King	And I'm sure we know who we have to thank.

The Lady-in-waiting cowers

	I think I would like our Lady-in-waiting
	Fried to a crisp on a red-hot grating.
Lady	Have pity, sire!
King	He was in our grasp — and you can't find the place!
	It's like hunting a shaggy dog on a wild goose chase!

He exits with the Officer

Lady	Oh Majesty, Majesty, Majesty please ...
	I'm at your mercy. I'm on my knees.

The Queen helps her up

Queen	Get up. He doesn't mean it ...
Lady	Oh dear ... oh dear ...
Queen	But what he just said gave me an idea.
	"Hunting a shaggy dog". Hunters follow a trail.
	We'll do the same — and catch that soldier without fail!

They exit and there is a dissolve to:

SCENE 6

The Attic

The Soldier is in uniform. He has a big book

Soldier I thought I'd come up to the attic again and have a good think. I won't send for her tonight. She says she'll give up being a Princess for my sake and I can't have that. It wouldn't be fair. It wouldn't. So that's it. (*He sings softly*)

Song: It's Over (Reprise)

It's over, it's over,
Our love could never last,
It's over, it's over ...
It'll soon be in the past ...

(*Speaking*) Mind you — there is one other way. Instead of her stopping being a Princess, I could try harder to turn myself into a Prince. I have tried already. I got this book. I was told it was all about good manners and how to behave in a princely way. There's only one problem. I can read my name and a few names of battles, but that's all. I can't read properly. Don't sneer. I'm not the only one. Reading's hard ... (*He tries the first words*) Ke ... ii ... nnn ... geh ... zzz ...aaah ... nnn ... deh ... It's no use! (*Pause*) I know. I won't send for the Princess, but I'll just send for the dog — just for a bit of company. Shall I? All right then, let's do the spell ... (*He gets tinder box*)
One and two ...
Two and three ...
Tinder box, tinder box,
Spark for me!
One!

He strikes once. There are flashes of sparks and a dog howl

The Dog with eyes as big as saucers appears

Dog What is your wish, oh master?
Soldier Nothing much. I just wanted to see you. You could sit with me like normal dogs do. I mean, you aren't just a magic dog are you? You do all the things dogs do, don't you? D'you run in rivers and come out and shake yourself over everyone so they get soaked?
Dog No, master.
Soldier Do you cock your leg up against trees?
Dog No, master.
Soldier Do you nip round the park sniffing other dogs' bottoms?
Dog No, master.
Soldier What do you do?
Dog I stay under the earth and wait for command, master.
Soldier That's no life for a dog! Well sit here a bit. Maybe you can get the

Princess later. But first I've got to improve myself. (*He picks up the book*)
I wish I could read!

There is a magical sound. The Soldier stares at the book and slowly realizes he can read

Here! What's this? I *can* read. You've done it! I can read. (*Reading*) "Kings
and Princes never belch after meals or pick their teeth ... " I can read!! At
this rate I'll be asking the Princess to marry me!

The Dog makes a sound, pleased. The Lights fade as there is a dissolve to:

SCENE 7

The Copper Tower

*The Queen is waiting impatiently. She holds a silk bag (containing grains of
wheat), half hidden*

The Narrators appear

Narrators But the soldier reckoned without the Queen,
              The cleverest queen that's ever been.
              She could do more than ride in a golden carriage.
              And she was determined to stop her daughter's marriage.

The Narrators disappear

*The Princess enters in her night-dress, brushing her hair. She looks for
something in the room. The Lady-in-waiting enters after her, fussing*

Queen   (*coolly*)
              You seem pleased with yourself ...
Princess It's Christmas time — or very nearly ...
Queen   Remember that I love you dearly.
              Before you go to your bedroom and put out the light
              Come back and kiss your mother good-night.

The Princess finds what she was looking for and starts to leave

Princess I will!

She exits

The Queen is suspicious of her daughter's cheerful mood. She grabs the Lady-in-waiting before she has a chance to follow the Princess out

Queen   Listen! Carefully. I've a plan that I think rather neat.
           I've filled this silken bag with small grains of wheat. *(She pours*
             some wheat from the bag into her hand, then pours it back)
           We pin the bag on her night-dress without her knowing.
           Then when she rides out — just as she's going —
           I'll snip a hole in the bag so the grains leave a trail.
           Which we'll follow. Find the soldier, and put him in jail.
Lady   You mean all those little grains of wheat
           Will pop out, one by one, along the street?
           How brilliant, Your Majesty — I wish I was bright.
Queen   Just concentrate and get the thing right!
           Take the bag and hide it behind the chair.
           When she comes back I'll talk to her — over there.
           You'll have your chance when she's turned to me ...
           Pin the bag to her dress, and don't let her see!

The Princess enters

           Ah ... she's here ...
Lady   Oh yes ... oh dear ...

The Lady-in-waiting tries to sit nonchalantly on a chair, hiding the bag. The Queen manœuvres the Princess into position deftly. The Princess kisses her mother, then makes a big show of yawning

Princess   Well I think it's time that I shut my eyes ...
Queen   Yes of course — I'm sure you're very wise
           And I hope that you go off to sleep like a log
           And don't go riding on any stray dog!

The Lady-in-waiting, crawling up behind the Princess with the bag, is left stranded as the Princess moves suddenly away

Princess   That was just a dream! It's too absurd ...
Queen   I know — I didn't believe a single word.

The Lady makes another attempt but the Princess moves again

Princess   Oh look at the moon — what a beautiful Christmassy sight.
Queen   Yes — I could stand here, *quite still*, and stare all night.
               Don't move! Such scenes are all too rare ...

The Lady-in-waiting tries again to pin the bag on the hem of the Princess's night-gown, but the Princess swings round, yawning and catches her on the floor

Princess   Oh! What on earth are you doing down there?
Queen   I think she's been praying ...

The Lady-in-waiting hastily puts her hands together

Lady   That's right — praying — yes, yes, yes!
               God bless the King and Queen and our dear Princess!
Princess   Thank you — amen. (*She yawns*)
               Oh I'll sleep and sleep and sleep again!

   She exits

Lady   I'm sorry, Your Majesty. She wouldn't stay near!
               I couldn't do it. Oh dear! Oh dear!
Queen   I put crushed poppy in her drink. She'll sleep sound.
               You can pin it on her nightie before she comes round ...

The Lights fade to a Black-out. Dissolve to:

SCENE 8

Outside the Inn

The Soldier, very formal, in uniform, practises his proposal

Soldier Your Highness, the common soldier humbly begs to propose a state
of matrimony between us. (*He shakes his head*) No. Sounds as if I was
declaring war! Try again. Your Highness, may I humbly ask for your hand
in marriage? No — I'm not humble. I'm a soldier. (*He becomes more
forthright*) Princess Sigrid — that's better — Princess Sigrid, I'll ask you
straight. I love you — will you be my mate? Hmmm. Not bad. Where's that
dog? I sent him for her ages ago. Has something happened?

The Lights fade on him as he practises his proposal

*The Lights become eerie as the moon shines on the Dog, who enters,
carrying the sleeping Princess*

The Narrators appear

Narrators How cruel was the brightness of that night,
As the Princess rode her final ride ...
And grain by grain in the white moonlight,
The wheat left a trail that nothing could hide.
Where, oh where, as he padded along
Was the Dog's sixth sense that something was wrong?

The Dog does pause a moment and turns to look back

But he never heard — and never saw
The one grain, two grains, three grains, four
That would lead the King to the Soldier's door.

The Dog brings the Princess to the Soldier

Soldier Princess!

She wakes as he helps her down

Princess I'm here! Oh don't tell me I slept all the way?
Soldier (*to the Dog*)
You did well. Now leave us. I've something to say.

The Dog makes a disappointed sound and exits into the inn

Princess ...
Princess Yes?
Soldier Well — it's — it's — I'm a bit tongue-tied ...
Princess Go on: it's ...
Soldier It's cold out here. Let's go inside.

They exit into the inn

*The King, Queen, Lady-in-waiting and Officer creep in, following the trail
of grains*

Narrators	Just then the King and Queen and their train
	Came following the trail of grain ...
Officer	There's another ...
Queen	And there!
Lady	And there!
King	Let him get away this time if he dare!
Narrators	And now the trail of grains has stopped,
	At the Soldier's door the last grain had dropped.

The Narrators disappear

The Officer knocks at the door

Officer	Open up in the name of the King!
Queen	Break the door down, you stupid thing!

The Officer breaks down the door

Mrs Pin and Boots enter, alarmed by the commotion

Mrs Pin	Whatever is happening? What's going on?
Officer	We want the soldier!
Boots	I think he's gone ...
Officer	Hear this in the name of the King of the Danes ...
	Whoever protects him will end in chains!
Queen	I know he's here. We're getting warm.
King	We are looking for a man in soldier's uniform.
Mrs Pin	One of our guests might have a uniform. I'll go and see ...

Boots is disgusted by her treachery

King	That's him! Bring the cur to me!

But the Soldier enters to meet them. He stands to attention and salutes

Soldier	Your Majesty, you needn't drag me out.
	I'm your common soldier — and I know what duty is about.
	It's true I called the Princess to me here ...
	But no harm came to her — have no fear.
Queen	The lying wretch!
Lady	The fiend!

| King | You cheeky pup! |
| Queen | Where is she? What have you done? |

The Princess enters. She stands by the Soldier

Princess	I'm here — and I'm not going to hide.
	My place from now on is at his side.
King	Not when he hangs it isn't! (*He challenges the Soldier*)
	Soldier, do you plead guilty or not guilty — say!
Soldier	Well ...
King	Guilty! It's settled — we'll hang him today.
Princess	No!
Queen	Yes!
Soldier	But I need to get ready before you do it ...
King	We hang you by the neck. That's all there is to it!
Soldier	But I'm a soldier. I demand to be shot ...
King	You'll have the rope. It's all we've got.
Soldier	But it's Christmas. I'll miss the Yuletide feast.
Queen	We'll have that when you're hung, you awful beast!

The Officer takes the Soldier away, followed by the Royal party

| Boots | They can't! They can't! He done nothin' wrong ... |
| Mrs Pin | He's a villain. I knew it. I knew it all along! |

Mrs Pin and Boots exit into the inn

The Dog with eyes as big as saucers enters

Dog	Master, master — send for me,
	Strike the tinder box wherever you may be,
	And from the hall below the tree,
	The dogs will come obediently!

Dissolve to:

SCENE 9

A Gaol near the gallows

The Hangman constructs the gallows. People hurry across the stage with Christmas hampers, gifts and decorations, singing as they go

Song: Ding Dong Merrily On High

All   Ding dong merrily on high
We're going to hang the Soldier!
And eat our Christmas pie
Before it all goes cold-yer!
Glor—or—or—or—or—ia
We're going to hang the Soldier!

The Company disperse

The Officer enters with the Soldier and locks him in gaol

Officer   *(speaking)*
There's no escape. You needn't try.
And there's the gallows for hanging you high.

He exits

Soldier   Christmas — and here I am in gaol,
And they're going to hang me up without fail.
If only I could call the dog to open these locks,
But you know what I've done? I've forgot the tinder box!
It's no use. My fate is sealed.
Soldier! You're on your last battlefield ...

Boots enters and walks past

         Hey Boots!
Boots   Who is it?
Soldier   Me!
Boots   The Soldier ... oh hell!
Soldier   Where were you running to, pell mell?
Boots   I'll be hung for talking to you ...
Soldier   I'll be hung whether you don't or you do.
I bet you're going to see the King
And stand by the gallows to see me swing.
Boots   I knew you as a soldier. I knew you as a toff.
I knew you as a friend. I have to see you off ...
Soldier   Well it won't happen yet. It can't start without me.
There's something you could get that I don't have about me.

My tinder box. I can't pay you proper.
Only in copper. (*He offers four copper coins*)

Boots   Done! To me that's quite a sum! (*He pockets the coins*)

There is the faint sound of a slow drum roll

Soldier   Run! For now I hear the hanging drum ...

Boots exits

The Officer enters the prison cell

Officer   By order of the King, say your last prayer.
I'm here with the Hangman to take you there.
Soldier   As for Our Heavenly Father, He knows what I feel.
As for the King — I want to make an appeal.
Officer   Too late for appeals. The gallows is ready.
Soldier   Then do something for me to help me be steady.
Take a message to someone. I'll soon be dead.
Tell the Princess I loved her. I never properly said.
Officer   Slow march!

The Officer marches the Soldier in front of him, towards the gallows. The Soldier tries to delay

Soldier   A moment. I came over all dizzy ...
(*Aside*) Where is that Boots? Come on! Where is he?

They march on

Boots races in

Boots   Sir! Sir! The King is coming! (*Pointing*) There!
Officer   Where?

As the Officer is distracted, Boots slips the tinder box to the Solider

Boots   Here — your tinder box.
Soldier   Thanks Boots. I shan't forget ...

The Officer and the Soldier reach the gallows

The King, Queen and Lady-in-waiting enter. The Company assemble

King   Now everybody — are we all set?
Officer   Yes, Your Majesty.
King   Let's get it over. No more delay ...
Soldier   (*from the scaffold*)
              Your Majesty, I hope you won't say me "nay"
              If I have one last wish ...
Officer   It's usual, sire ...
King   Usual? Pish!
Queen   It's the custom. Do it dear. Don't wrangle.
Soldier   I'd like one last smoke before I dangle.
              I've got my tinder box to light it well ...
              (*Aside*) Children, get ready to say the spell!
King   Wish granted. But hurry — we want to eat.
Soldier   Now children, the spell, with me, repeat:

The children join in the spell

              One and two ...
              Two and three ...
              Tinder box, tinder box,
              Spark for me!
Soldier   (*striking the box*)
              One ... two ... three!

Thunderclap. Sparks. Dog howls

  All three Dogs appear

The King, Queen, Hangman and Officer react with fear

Queen   We're bewitched!
King   What are these things?
Dogs   We serve our master. Death to Kings!

  The King, Queen, Hangman and Officer flee

  The Narrators appear

Narrators And the King and Queen were flung up to the sky,
               Touching the clouds, they went so high.

	And when they fell, like pots and crocks, they shattered
	Into little pieces that flew and scattered.
Boots	And the people shouted: "Our soldier shall be King
	And marry the Princess and have everything!"

The Princess and Lady-in-waiting enter

Soldier   Your Highness, I've loved you since you came sleeping through
the snow.
Princess Sigrid — will you marry me?

Dramatic pause. We guess the answer

Princess   No.
Soldier   You said "No"!
Princess   I love you — but now I'm wide awake
And I say "no" for your own sake;
For see how harshly you behave,
Sending my parents to their grave.
Soldier   But look what they did! They shut you away!
And as for me, they'd have hung me today ...
What should we do? Let them off with a fine?
Princess   They're all the parents I have. They're bad — but they're mine.
The Dogs broke them to pieces, ten times ten.
I want their magic to put them together again.
Soldier   Saucer Eyes! Can it be done?
Dog   Yes, master ...
Princess   You see — it can!
Soldier   But that's another story.
Ours began when I came marching back from the wars
It ends when we marry ...
But after that — everything you want is yours!
Once more I ask: will you marry me, Princess?
Princess   To begin that other story, I answer ——

She gets the children to say it with her:

YES!

A feast and a Christmas tree are brought in

Narrators So they had both wedding cake *and* mince pies ...
And the magic Dogs just rolled their eyes!

The whole Company sings:

Song: Ding Dong Merrily on High (Reprise)

All   Ding dong merrily on high
               She's going to wed the Soldier
               And now we say goodbye
               Our story we have told yer
               Glor .. or .. or .. or .. or .. or .. ia!
               She's going to wed the Soldier.

Black-out

CURTAIN

It's over

Words and Music by Peter Whelan

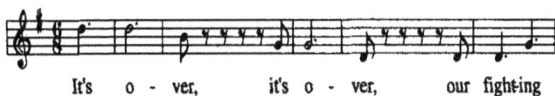

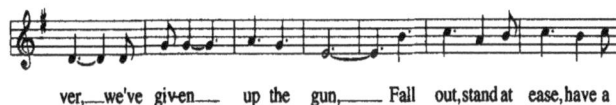

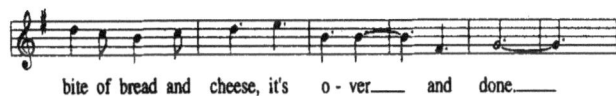

It's o - ver, it's o - ver, our fight-ing

days are gone,____ it's o - ver, the war is o - ver, we don't

know___ who's lost or won.____ It's o - ver it's o -

ver,___we've giv-en___ up the gun,____ Fall out, stand at ease, have a

bite of bread and cheese, it's o - ver____ and done.____

I'm rich

Music by John Kirkpatrick
Words by Peter Whelan

I'm rich, I'm rich, and all on ac-

count of that old witch, if

on-ly she'd said why, she would-n't have had to

die, still, I'm rich, I'm

rich, I'm rich, I'm rich, I'm

rich, I'm rich, I'm rich!

Where are you

Words and Music by Peter Whelan

Where are you___ my com-mon sol-dier___ as you

march___ to drum and fife?___ Will I take___ you for my

hus-band,___ will you have___ me for your wife?___

Oh where are you?___ where are you?___ Oh where, my

love, my life?___

Let's see your money first

Words and Music by Peter Whelan

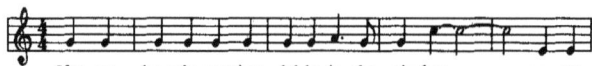

You can have the pret-tiest dol-ly in the win-dow,_____ you can

have the nic-est sweet-ies from the shelf,_____ and all those love-ly

things up-on the count-er,_____ you can have them wrapped and

keep them for your - self._____ You can go to town to all the fin-est

rest-'raunts,_____ and eat the tast-iest dish-es till you burst._____ But

just be-fore you do, some-one's going to say to you, 'Let's see your

mo-ney first.' Let's see your mo-ney, let's see your mo-ney,

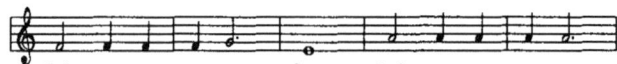

let's see your mo-ney first. Let's see your mo-ney,

let's see your mo-ney, let's see your mo-ney first.

Cophenhagen garden

Words and Music by Peter Whelan

In Co - pen - ha- gen,___ there is a gar-den,___ where you can

watch the ships go by. And wood- lands all a- bout,

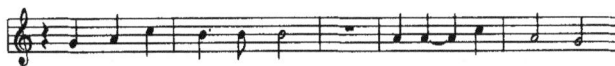

where chil-dren laugh and shout, un-der___ a bright blue

sky. In Co - pen - ha - gen,___ in that gar - den,___

we'll make___ our own sweet world, and no more will I be___

_ princess or roy-al- ty,___ your Co- pen - ha - gen girl.___

Ding dong merrily on high

Music - Trad

New words by Peter Whelan

Ding dong mer-ri-ly on high, we're going to hang the sol-dier, and

eat our Christ-mas___ pie, be - fore it all goes cold-yer!

Glo___

___ ri- a, we're going to hang the sol - dier.

FURNITURE AND PROPERTY LIST

ACT I
SCENE 1

Personal: **Soldier**: drum, pouches containing money, knapsack containing sausage, bit of rope, pipe, tobacco, fish hooks, bed-roll, hat and broken compass, spare long johns, pair of worn-out socks, scabbard with sword and liquorice root
Comrade: fife, belt

Off stage: Hollow oak tree

SCENE 2

Personal: **Witch**: stick, rope, apron

SCENE 3

Note: The **Dogs** appear in this scene

Off stage: Copper chest. *In it:* copper coins (**First Dog**)
Silver chest. *In it:* silver coins (**Second Dog**)
Gold chest. *In it:* gold coins (**Third Dog**)

SCENE 4

Strike: Gold chest

Set: Hollow tree. *In it:* tinder box

SCENE 5

Strike: Hollow tree

SCENE 6

Off stage: Hobby horse bike (**Man**)
Horn (**Officer**)
Roses (**Rose Seller**)
Tray. *On it:* gingerbread men (**Baker**)

Personal: **Soldier**: coins

SCENE 7

Personal:	**Scoff**: napkin

SCENE 8

Set:	Copper gate Gate
Off stage:	Bags and boxes (**Lady-in-waiting**)
Personal:	**Officer**: key

SCENE 9

Strike:	Gates
Set:	Four poster bed. *Under it:* money box containing coins
Off stage:	Breakfast trolley. *On it:* lots of food (**Mrs Pin** and **Scoff**) Boots and clothes (**Boots**)

SCENE 10

Strike:	Four poster bed Breakfast trolley
Set:	Copper chair Needlework box, home loom and knitting (with needles)

SCENE 11

Strike:	Copper chair Needlework box, etc.
Set:	Lanterns in trees Champagne and glasses (**Chorus**) Wheel of fortune (**Croupier**)
Off stage:	Champagne (**Scoff**) Sign: "Blue Moon"
Personal:	**Soldier**: money box containing coins **Widow**: stick

Strike:	Wheel of fortune Lanterns, trees, etc.
Off stage:	Tables and chairs (**Waiter**) Food (**Waiter**)

SCENE 13

Strike:	Tables and chairs, food, champagne, etc.
Set:	Dirty ragged blanket Soldier's uniform, drum, knapsack, sword, etc.
Off stage:	Soldier's old boots (**Boots**) Copper Tower

ACT II
SCENE 1

Note:	The **Dogs** appear in this scene
On stage:	Blanket
Off stage:	Food scraps, etc. wrapped in crumpled paper, water bottle (**Boots**) Bag of copper coins (**First Dog**) — to appear magically Bag of silver coins (**Second Dog**) — to appear magically Bag of gold coins (**Third Dog**) — to appear magically
Personal:	**Boots**: needle **Soldier**: knapsack containing items as per ACT I, SCENE 1 **and** tinder box

SCENE 2

Note:	The **First Dog** appears in this scene
Off stage:	Four poster bed (**Scoff** and **Twist**) Blanket (Soldier)
Personal:	**Soldier**: tinder box

SCENE 3

Strike:	Four poster bed
Off stage:	Thick toast (**Princess**)

SCENE 4

Note:	The **First Dog** appears in this scene
Personal:	**Lady-in-waiting**: chalk **First Dog**: chalk

SCENE 5

Nil

SCENE 6

Note:	The **First Dog** appears in this scene
Personal:	**Soldier**: book, tinder box

SCENE 7

Set:	Chair
Off stage:	Hairbrush (**Princess**)
Personal:	**Queen**: silk bag containing small grains of wheat

SCENE 8

Note:	The **First Dog** appears in this scene
Strike:	Chair
Set:	Door
Personal:	**Princess**: silk bag containing grains of wheat (attached to hem)

SCENE 9

Note:	The **Dogs** appear in this scene
Strike:	Door (broken)
Set:	Gallows, scaffold, etc. Goal
Off stage:	Christmas hampers, gifts, decorations (**Company**) Tinder box (**Boots**) Feast (**Company**) Christmas Tree (**Company**)
Personal:	**Officer**: key **Soldier**: copper, coins

LIGHTING PLOT

Practical fittings required: Nil
Various interior and exterior settings

ACT 1, SCENE 1

To open: Exterior lighting on Dust Road, evening

Cue 1   Music   (Page 3)
            The stage darkens a little, then crossfade to SCENE 2

ACT I, SCENE 2

To open: Exterior lighting on area around oak tree

Cue 2   The **Soldier** puts his head down and sleeps   (Page 3)
            Stage darkens, then Witch's shadow falls across stage

ACT I, SCENE 3

To open: Interior lighting in underground hall, lamp effect

Cue 3   **Soldier**: "Let's try my luck next door."   (Page 8)
            Lighting change as **Soldier** *moves back into hall*

Cue 4   The **Soldier** gets the audience to shout "Silver".   (Page 9)
            Lighting change as second **Dog** *disappears*

Cue 5   The **Narrators** disappear   (Page 10)
            Quick black-out; lights up to reveal huge eyes of third **Dog**

Cue 6   The **Soldier** opens the golden chest   (Page 10)
            Golden light effect around chest

Cue 7   The **Soldier** tugs on the rope   (Page 11)
            Lighting change, then crossfade to SCENE 4

ACT I, SCENE 4

To open: Exterior lighting around oak tree

Cue 8	**Soldier**: "Tell the truth ..." *Dawn effect*	(Page 13)
Cue 9	**Witch**: "The dawn! The sun!" *Stream of sunlight*	(Page 13)
Cue 10	The **Soldier** sweeps at the **Witch** with his sword *Blinding flash of light*	(Page 13)
Cue 11	The **Witch** exits, screaming *Gentle sunrise effect*	(Page 13)

ACT I, SCENE 5

To open: Interior lighting on Royal Palace

ACT I, SCENE 6

To open: Exterior lighting on Copenhagen

ACT I, SCENE 7

To open: Interior lighting on lobby of the Inn

Cue 12	The **Soldier** spills gold before **Mrs Pin** and friends *Gilded light plays about them*	(Page 21)

ACT I, SCENE 8

To open: Exterior lighting on Copenhagen

ACT I, SCENE 9

To open: Interior lighting around four poster bed

ACT I, SCENE 10

To open: Interior lighting on Copper Tower

ACT I, SCENE 11

To open: Exterior lighting on Pleasure Gardens; silvery, snowy effect

Cue 13	**Soldier**: " ... I must eat soon." *Light on "Blue Moon" sign as it arrives, then crossfade to* SCENE 12	(Page 29)

ACT I, Scene 12

To open: Interior lighting on Nightclub

ACT I, Scene 13

To open: Interior lighting on Attic, bare and cold

Cue 14   **Soldier**: "She needs cheering up."   (Page 34)
            Lights up on Copper Tower

Cue 15   The **Soldier** and the **Princess** continue tapping   (Page 36)
            Fade

Cue 16   Silence   (Page 36)
            Black-out

ACT II, Scene 1

To open: Interior lighting on Attic

ACT II, Scene 2

To open: Interior lighting on area around four poster bed

Cue 17   **Soldier**: "Was that him? Is he coming back?"   (Page 44)
            Lights grow for **Princess**'s *entrance; pearly pools of moonlight*
            to denote move to night-time exterior

Cue 18   The **Soldier** salutes, sadly   (Page 45)
            Lights fade to black then rise on Scene 3

ACT II, Scene 3

To open: Interior lighting on Copper Tower

Cue 19   **Lady**: "Oh dear! Oh dear!"   (Page 47)
            Lights fade to black then rise on Scene 4

ACT II, Scene 4

To open: Exterior night lighting on entrance to the Inn

Cue 20   The **Dog** exits. Music   (Page 49)
            Light grows from the inn door for entry of **Soldier** *and* **Princess**

Cue 21   The **Princess** and **Dog** start to exit   (Page 50)
            Start to fade, then crossfade to SCENE 5

ACT II, SCENE 5

To open: Exterior dawn effect lighting on entrance to the Inn

ACT II, SCENE 6

To open: Interior lighting on Attic

Cue 22   **Soldier**: " ... asking the Princess to marry me!"   (Page 54)
            Lights fade and crossfade to SCENE 7

ACT II, SCENE 7

To open: Interior lighting on Copper Tower

Cue 23   **Queen**: " ... before she comes round ..."   (Page 56)
            Fade to black-out, then bring up on SCENE 8

ACT II, SCENE 8

To open: Exterior lighting on an area outside the Inn

Cue 24   **Soldier**: "Has something happened?"   (Page 57)
            Fade lights on **Soldier**

Cue 25   **Dog** and **Princess** enter   (Page 57)
            Bring up eerie light, moonshine effect

ACT II, SCENE 9

To open: Interior lighting on Gaol and surrounding area

Cue 26   **Company** (*singing*): "She's going to wed the Soldier."   (Page 64)
            Final black-out

EFFECTS PLOT

Note: All three Dogs are treated as "characters", but cues for noises from the Dogs are given here, as if they were effects. It is up to the director whether the noises are implemented from the sound box or — at least in the case of the First Dog, Saucer Eyes — performed by the actors live on stage. Music cues are given, though they may be performed live by an onstage band.

ACT I
SCENE 1

Cue 1   As the **Narrators** begin the story   (Page 1)
Church bells; fade a few minutes into the scene

Cue 2   **Soldier**: "Well, I'll have to find somewhere."   (Page 3)
Music; fade after SCENE 2 *opens*

SCENE 2

Cue 3   Tap, tap, tap, off, as the **Witch** approaches   (Page 3)
Music

Cue 4   The tree moves off   (Page 6)
Music; fade as SCENE 3 *opens*

SCENE 3

Cue 5   **Soldier**: "I'll show him the Witch's apron."   (Page 7)
Echoing "mmmmaammmm" sound (from the **First Dog***)*

Cue 6   The **Dog** rolls his eyes   (Page 7)
Mystical sounds

Cue 7   **Soldier**: "I want to shake your paw, sir."   (Page 7)
Magical breathing dog sounds

Cue 8   **Soldier**: "I'll just take that much, thank you."   (Page 7)
Another "mmmmaammmm" sound

Cue 9   **Soldier**: "I'm going next door."   (Page 7)
Happy, friendly sound from **Dog**

Cue 10	**Soldier**: "Will you get off it please?"	(Page 7)
	More happy sounds from the **Dog**	
Cue 11	**Soldier**: "Off that apron!"	(Page 7)
	Happy, booming bark from the **Dog**	
Cue 12	When someone (audience or **Soldier**) says "Copper".	(Page 8)
	Respectful howl from the **Dog**	
Cue 13	**Soldier**: "Hey — that got him. Copper!"	(Page 8)
	The **Dog** *howls again*	
Cue 14	The **Soldier** spreads the apron on the ground with a flourish	(Page 9)
	Loud, deep hound-like howl from **Second Dog**	
Cue 15	The **Soldier** shows the **Third Dog** the apron	(Page 10)
	Very loud howl from **Third Dog**	
Cue 16	**Soldier**: "Say the word with me: 'Gold'."	(Page 11)
	Even louder howl from the **Dog**	

SCENE 4

No cues

SCENE 5

No cues

SCENE 6

Cue 17	At opening of scene	(Page 17)
	Clocks strike, band playing (the music may be performed live)	

SCENE 7

No cues

SCENE 8

No cues

SCENE 9

No cues

SCENE 10

No cues

SCENE 11

Cue 18   At scene opening   (Page 28)
             Music for polka

SCENE 12

No cues

SCENE 13

No cues

ACT II
SCENE 1

Cue 19   **Boots**: "Would I put a man in prison?"   (Page 39)
             Very faint sound of a lark

Cue 20   The **Soldier** strikes the tinder box once   (Page 40)
             A great doggy breathing, panting sound, getting louder and louder

Cue 21   **Dog (Saucer Eyes)**: "Yes, master!"   (Page 40)
             Musical howl from Dog

Cue 22   The **Soldier** strikes the tinder box twice   (Page 40)
             *Deep howl from **Second Dog**, off*

Cue 23   The **Soldier** strikes the tinder box three times (Page 41)
             *Deeper howl from **Third Dog**, off*

Cue 24   **Soldier**: " ... I just strike the tinder box?" (Page 41)
             *Voice effect from all three **Dogs**: "Yes, master!", then great
                 howling and barking*

SCENE 2

Cue 25   The **Soldier** strikes the tinder box once   (Page 44)
             *Cosmic dog panting (**First Dog**)*

Cue 26   The **Soldier** kisses the **Princess**   (Page 45)
             Magical humming sound

No cues

Cue 27   **Narrators**: " ... doggy smile he smiles ..."   (Page 49)
Happy sound from **First Dog**

Cue 28   **First Dog**: "They'll never know which door is yours!"   (Page 49)
Satisfied dog howl from **First Dog**

Cue 29   **First Dog** exits   (Page 49)
Music

No cues

Cue 30   The **Soldier** strikes the tinder box once   (Page 53)
Dog howl from **First Dog**, *off*

Cue 31   **Soldier**: "I wish I could read!"   (Page 54)
Magical sound

Cue 32   **Soldier**: " ... the Princess to marry me!"   (Page 54)
Happy sound from **First Dog**

No cues

Cue 33   **Soldier**: "I've something to say."   (Page 57)
Disappointed sound from **Dog** *as it exits*

Cue 34   **Boots**: "To me that's quite a sum!"   (Page 61)
Slow drum roll, off (this may be performed live if there is a band)

Cue 35   **Soldier**: "One ... two ... three!"   (Page 62)
Thunderclap, dog howls

www.ingramcontent.com/pod-product-compliance
Lightning Source LLC
LaVergne TN
LVHW051756080426
835511LV00018B/3332